Penetration Testing for Network Security

A Hacker's Perspective
Simulating cyberattacks to
strengthen network defenses

THOMPSON CARTER

Table of Content

TABLE OF CONTENTS

Introduction

In today's fast-paced digital world, networks are the backbone of all communication, from powering businesses to enabling IoT devices and 5G technologies. As the demand for higher speeds, greater reliability, and more efficient operations increases, managing networks has become a more complex and time-consuming task. Traditional methods of network management, largely reliant on manual configuration and intervention, are no longer sufficient to meet the growing needs of modern networks. This is where **network automation** steps in, revolutionizing how we configure, manage, and maintain our network infrastructures.

Network automation involves the use of technology to automate network management tasks such as configuration, monitoring, troubleshooting, and optimization, reducing the need for human intervention. By adopting automation, network administrators can streamline operations, increase consistency, reduce errors, and ensure that networks perform optimally. With the introduction of Python as the primary language for network automation, the process has become even more accessible and powerful. Python, known for its simplicity, versatility, and rich ecosystem of libraries, has emerged as a go-to tool for automating a wide range of network management tasks.

This book, **"Network Automation with Python: A Comprehensive Guide to Automating Network Management and Operations,"** is designed to provide an in-depth exploration of network automation using Python, from the foundational concepts to advanced implementation strategies. Whether you are new to network automation or are looking to expand your knowledge and skills, this book will serve as your guide to harnessing the power of Python in the world of network management.

Why Network Automation is Essential

The increasing complexity of networks, the rise of cloud computing, the proliferation of IoT devices, and the emergence of technologies like **5G** are all contributing to a rapidly changing networking landscape. Networks must support more devices, more applications, and more data than ever before. To keep up with this demand, automation is no longer optional—it is essential. Manual configuration and maintenance of network devices, which were once manageable, now lead to inefficiencies, errors, and security vulnerabilities.

Automating network management brings numerous benefits, including:

- **Increased Efficiency**: Automation speeds up tasks that would otherwise take hours to complete manually. Tasks like configuration updates, performance monitoring, and backups can be executed quickly, without human intervention.

- **Reduced Human Error**: Manual configuration is prone to errors, whether due to oversight, misconfiguration, or inconsistent execution. Automation eliminates many of these risks by ensuring that configurations and actions are consistent and accurate.

- **Enhanced Scalability**: As network infrastructures grow in size and complexity, managing these networks manually becomes unsustainable. Network automation allows organizations to scale their network operations seamlessly without additional overhead or complexity.

- **Proactive Network Management**: With the power of automation, network management moves from being reactive (responding to issues as they occur) to proactive (anticipating and addressing issues before they become critical). Automation tools can monitor network performance, identify bottlenecks, and even predict potential failures before they occur.

Why Python?

Python has become the dominant programming language for network automation due to its simplicity and extensive support for network management tools. As a high-level, interpreted language, Python is easy to learn, read, and maintain, making it an ideal choice for network engineers and administrators. In addition, Python's rich ecosystem of libraries and frameworks, such as **Netmiko**, **Nornir**, **Napalm**, and **PySNMP**, makes it highly adaptable for automating tasks across various network devices, from routers and switches to firewalls and load balancers.

Python also offers compatibility with popular automation platforms such as **Ansible** and **SaltStack**, allowing for seamless integration with existing network automation workflows. Furthermore, Python is an open-source language, which means that it is continually evolving and supported by a thriving community. This ensures that new tools, libraries, and best practices are always available to help network engineers stay ahead of the curve.

What You'll Learn in This Book

This book covers the full spectrum of network automation, from the foundational concepts to advanced techniques, with a strong emphasis on Python's capabilities. You'll learn how to automate network configuration, monitoring, troubleshooting, and security tasks, enabling you to create fully automated network management solutions.

Some key topics covered include:

- **The Basics of Network Automation**: An introduction to network automation concepts, tools, and why automation is critical for modern network management.
- **Python Fundamentals for Network Automation**: A comprehensive overview of Python's syntax and libraries specifically tailored for network automation. You'll learn how to use Python to interact with network devices, retrieve data, and apply configurations.
- **Network Configuration and Management**: Learn how to automate the configuration of network devices, including routers, switches, firewalls, and

load balancers. You'll also explore best practices for configuration management and version control.

- **Network Monitoring and Performance Optimization**: Understand how to automate network monitoring tasks such as performance checks, traffic analysis, and uptime monitoring, and how to optimize network performance using automation.

- **Security Best Practices in Network Automation**: Learn how to secure your network automation scripts and manage authentication, authorization, and access control to prevent unauthorized access and ensure safe automation.

- **Scaling Automation for Large Networks**: Explore techniques for scaling your automation solutions to handle large, complex networks with thousands of devices. You'll learn how to automate network tasks at scale while maintaining reliability and performance.

- **Integrating with AI and Next-Gen Technologies**: Understand how Python can be used in conjunction with AI, machine learning, and predictive analytics to further enhance network automation and move towards intelligent, self-healing networks.

Real-World Applications and Examples

This book is not just theoretical; it includes practical examples and real-world use cases to show you how to apply network automation in various scenarios. From automating routine network tasks like configuration backups and performance monitoring to advanced topics like integrating AI-driven automation and managing large-scale networks, each chapter is designed to build your knowledge and skillset progressively.

The examples are structured to be easy to follow, even if you have limited experience with Python or network automation. As you progress, you will gradually gain the confidence to tackle increasingly complex network management tasks and leverage Python's full potential in your daily work.

Who Should Read This Book?

This book is designed for network engineers, administrators, and anyone involved in network management and automation. It is suitable for professionals at various levels of experience:

- **Beginners**: If you're new to Python or network automation, this book will provide you with a strong foundation in both Python programming and network automation principles.

- **Intermediate Users**: If you already have experience with Python and networking, this book will help you deepen your knowledge and expand your skillset by providing more advanced automation techniques and best practices.

- **Experienced Network Engineers**: For seasoned professionals, this book offers insights into scaling network automation, integrating advanced technologies like AI, and optimizing large networks through automation.

Why This Book is Important

Network automation is no longer a luxury—it's a necessity. As networks become larger, more complex, and more integral to business operations, the need for automation will continue to grow. By mastering Python for network automation, you are future-proofing your career and equipping yourself with the tools necessary to thrive in an increasingly automated world.

The practical skills you gain from this book will enable you to automate your network management tasks, reduce manual errors, improve efficiency, and enhance the reliability and security of your network infrastructure. Whether you're managing a small local area network (LAN) or a global wide area network (WAN), Python will empower you to automate processes, optimize performance, and stay ahead of the curve in the fast-evolving world of network management.

Let's Get Started!

Are you ready to dive into the world of network automation? Let's begin by exploring the fundamentals of network automation and how Python can transform the way you manage your network. With the knowledge and skills you gain from this book, you'll be well on your way to building the next generation of network automation solutions.

CHAPTER 1

INTRODUCTION TO NETWORK AUTOMATION

Overview of Network Automation and Its Significance

Network automation refers to the process of using technology to automatically configure, manage, and monitor network systems. It reduces the need for manual intervention in network operations, improving efficiency and reliability. As networks become more complex, automation has become essential to ensure that network tasks are completed quickly, consistently, and without errors.

The significance of network automation lies in its ability to handle routine tasks such as configuration management, performance monitoring, and fault detection, freeing up network administrators to focus on higher-level tasks. It also ensures that network changes are applied in a standardized and repeatable manner, reducing human error and minimizing downtime.

In today's digital landscape, networks are expanding rapidly with the growth of cloud computing, IoT devices, and remote work setups. As a result, maintaining these networks without automation becomes increasingly difficult, which is why many businesses turn to automation to meet their operational needs.

Benefits of Using Automation in Network Management

1. **Increased Efficiency and Speed:** Automation accelerates network management processes by handling repetitive tasks like configuration changes, software updates, and security patches without the need for manual input. This leads to faster response times and less downtime.

2. **Reduced Human Error:** Manual network configuration is prone to human errors, which can lead to outages or security vulnerabilities. Automation eliminates this risk by ensuring that tasks are executed consistently and correctly each time.

3. **Cost Savings:** By automating routine tasks, businesses can save on labor costs and reduce the

need for manual interventions. Additionally, automated systems can identify issues before they become critical, potentially saving money on emergency repairs.

4. **Scalability:** As networks grow, managing them manually becomes more challenging. Automation allows businesses to scale their network operations seamlessly without adding significant manual workload or resources.

5. **Improved Security:** Automation can help enforce security policies by automatically applying updates, patches, and configurations. It can also monitor the network for anomalies and potential threats in real time, ensuring that any security breaches are detected quickly.

6. **Consistency and Standardization:** Automation ensures that all network configurations are standardized and adhere to best practices, which is particularly important for large and distributed networks. This uniformity reduces configuration drift and makes troubleshooting easier.

Introduction to Python as a Powerful Tool for Automation

Python has become one of the most popular programming languages for network automation due to its simplicity, readability, and extensive library support. It allows network engineers and administrators to create custom scripts to automate various network tasks, making it easier to manage complex networks.

Some of the reasons Python is an ideal tool for network automation include:

1. **Ease of Use:** Python's syntax is intuitive and easy to understand, even for beginners. This makes it a great choice for network professionals who may not have extensive programming experience.

2. **Wide Range of Libraries:** Python offers numerous libraries specifically designed for network automation, including **Netmiko**, **NAPALM**, and **Paramiko**. These libraries simplify the process of interacting with networking devices and automate tasks like device configuration, data collection, and performance monitoring.

3. **Cross-Platform Compatibility:** Python can run on multiple platforms, such as Windows, Linux, and

macOS. This makes it versatile and suitable for use in a variety of network environments.

4. **Integration with Other Tools:** Python can easily integrate with other network management tools and protocols such as SNMP (Simple Network Management Protocol), REST APIs, and SSH. This allows users to create sophisticated automation workflows that interact with existing network infrastructure.

5. **Active Community and Support:** Python has a large and active community of developers, which means that support, tutorials, and resources are readily available for those learning or troubleshooting automation tasks.

This chapter sets the foundation for understanding how network automation can improve the efficiency and reliability of network management. By using Python, network professionals can automate a wide range of tasks, ensuring their networks run smoothly and securely. The following chapters will delve deeper into specific tools and techniques for implementing automation in different aspects of network management.

CHAPTER 2

UNDERSTANDING NETWORKING BASICS

Key Networking Concepts and Protocols

To successfully automate network management, it's crucial to understand the foundational concepts that make up the network infrastructure. Below are some key networking concepts and protocols every network automation engineer should be familiar with:

1. **IP Addressing (Internet Protocol Addressing):**
   o **IPv4**: The most commonly used IP version, consisting of 32 bits, represented in four octets (e.g., 192.168.1.1). It provides approximately 4.3 billion unique addresses, but due to the rapid growth of connected devices, its availability is limited.
   o **IPv6**: The successor to IPv4, using 128-bit addresses (e.g., 2001:0db8:85a3:0000:0000:8a2e:0370:7334). IPv6 can accommodate an almost limitless

number of unique addresses, making it essential for future network growth.

2. **Subnetting:**

   o Subnetting divides a network into smaller, more manageable pieces called subnets. This process helps organize networks, improves security, and optimizes network performance by reducing congestion and collisions.

3. **Routing:**

   o Routing is the process of determining the best path for data to travel across a network. Routers use routing tables to make these decisions based on factors such as IP address and network topology.

   o **Dynamic Routing**: Protocols like **OSPF (Open Shortest Path First)** and **BGP (Border Gateway Protocol)** automatically adjust the routes based on network conditions.

   o **Static Routing**: Involves manually configuring routes, which can be useful in smaller networks or when specific route control is needed.

4. **DNS (Domain Name System):**

   o DNS is the system that translates human-readable domain names (like www.example.com) into IP addresses (like 192.168.1.1). This allows users to

21

access websites and services without needing to memorize numeric IP addresses.

5. **DHCP (Dynamic Host Configuration Protocol):**
   o DHCP automatically assigns IP addresses to devices on a network, eliminating the need for manual configuration of each device's IP address. It simplifies network management by reducing the chances of IP conflicts.

6. **TCP/IP (Transmission Control Protocol/Internet Protocol):**
   o This suite of protocols forms the foundation of the internet. **TCP** ensures reliable communication by establishing connections and ensuring data is transmitted correctly, while **IP** handles addressing and routing the data to its destination.

7. **VLAN (Virtual Local Area Network):**
   o VLANs allow a network to be segmented into smaller, isolated sections, which improves security, traffic management, and performance. Devices on different VLANs cannot directly communicate without a router or Layer 3 switch to route traffic between them.

Common Network Devices and Their Roles

Network devices form the physical and logical components of a network, each with specific roles that help to maintain connectivity, security, and performance:

1. **Router:**
   - o   A router connects different networks (e.g., a local area network and the internet) and determines the best path for data to travel. Routers operate at Layer 3 (Network layer) of the OSI model and use routing tables to forward data packets based on their destination IP address.

2. **Switch:**
   - o   A switch is used within a single network to connect devices like computers, printers, and servers. Switches operate at Layer 2 (Data Link layer) of the OSI model and forward data based on MAC addresses. They efficiently handle local traffic within the same network, reducing congestion.

3. **Firewall:**
   - o   A firewall is a security device that monitors and controls incoming and outgoing network traffic based on predetermined security rules. Firewalls can be hardware-based or software-based and

help protect the network from unauthorized access, attacks, and malware.

4. **Access Point (AP):**

   o An access point allows wireless devices (laptops, smartphones, etc.) to connect to a wired network. It acts as a bridge between the wireless and wired portions of the network, extending the network's reach to mobile devices.

5. **Load Balancer:**

   o A load balancer distributes incoming network traffic across multiple servers to ensure no single server is overwhelmed. This improves the reliability and performance of applications, especially in high-traffic environments.

6. **Network Interface Card (NIC):**

   o A NIC is a hardware component that allows a device to connect to a network. It could be wired (Ethernet) or wireless (Wi-Fi). Each NIC has a unique MAC address that identifies it on the network.

7. **Gateway:**

   o A gateway connects two networks that use different protocols. In home networks, the router often acts as a gateway, allowing devices to connect to the internet (a different network from the local LAN).

Networking Terminology Every Automation Engineer Should Know

Understanding common networking terminology is essential for any automation engineer, especially when working with network configurations, monitoring, and automation scripts. Here are some key terms:

1. **Port:**
   o A port is a logical endpoint in a network where data is sent or received. It is identified by a number (e.g., port 80 for HTTP, port 443 for HTTPS). Ports help devices distinguish between different types of network traffic.

2. **Packet:**
   o A packet is a small unit of data transmitted over a network. Each packet contains data and information about its origin, destination, and sequence. Networking protocols like TCP/IP handle how packets are routed and assembled into larger data streams.

3. **Latency:**
   o Latency is the time it takes for data to travel from one point in the network to another. High latency can cause delays in communication, affecting

user experience, especially in real-time applications like video streaming or VoIP.

4. **Bandwidth:**

   o Bandwidth refers to the maximum amount of data that can be transmitted over a network connection in a given period, usually measured in bits per second (bps). Higher bandwidth results in faster data transmission.

5. **Throughput:**

   o Throughput is the actual rate at which data is successfully transmitted over the network, as opposed to the maximum potential bandwidth. It accounts for factors like latency, network congestion, and protocol overhead.

6. **Firewall Rules:**

   o These are the conditions set within a firewall to allow or block specific types of network traffic. They can be based on IP addresses, ports, protocols, or even specific applications.

7. **SNMP (Simple Network Management Protocol):**

   o SNMP is a protocol used to manage and monitor network devices like routers, switches, and firewalls. It helps automation engineers collect performance data and receive alerts when something goes wrong.

8. **Port Forwarding:**

o Port forwarding involves redirecting network traffic from one IP address and port to another. It's commonly used in home networks to allow external devices to access internal servers or services.

9. **Topology:**

o Topology refers to the physical and logical layout of a network. Common network topologies include star, ring, bus, and mesh. Understanding network topology is critical for effective automation and troubleshooting.

10. **QoS (Quality of Service):**

o QoS refers to the management of network resources to ensure optimal performance for critical applications. It involves prioritizing certain types of traffic, like VoIP or streaming video, over less time-sensitive traffic.

This chapter provides the foundational knowledge needed to understand networking principles. With these concepts in hand, network automation engineers can create effective scripts to automate configuration tasks, monitor performance, and address vulnerabilities more efficiently. As the chapters progress, you will learn how to use Python and other tools to automate these core networking tasks, creating streamlined and efficient workflows.

CHAPTER 3

SETTING UP PYTHON FOR NETWORK AUTOMATION

Installing Python and Necessary Packages

Before diving into network automation with Python, it's essential to set up your development environment. Python is a versatile and powerful tool for automating network tasks, but you need to ensure you have the right version of Python and necessary libraries installed.

1. **Installing Python:**
   - o **Step 1: Download Python**: The latest version of Python can be downloaded from the official Python website. It is recommended to use Python 3.x since it has several improvements over Python 2.x.
   - o **Step 2: Install Python**: Run the installer and make sure to check the box that says "Add Python to PATH" before clicking "Install Now." This ensures that Python can be accessed from the command line on your computer.

o **Step 3: Verify Installation**: Open a terminal or command prompt and type the following command to check if Python is installed:

```bash

python --version
```

If installed correctly, this will return the Python version number.

2. **Installing Required Packages:** Python has a vast ecosystem of libraries that simplify network automation tasks. The most common package manager for Python is **pip**, which is installed by default with Python.

Some essential packages for network automation include:

o **Netmiko**: A Python library that simplifies the process of automating network devices like routers, switches, and firewalls using SSH.

- Install Netmiko by running:

```bash

pip install netmiko
```

30

o **NAPALM**: A library designed to automate network devices through a uniform API, supporting various platforms like Cisco, Juniper, and Arista.

- Install NAPALM by running:

```bash

pip install napalm
```

o **Paramiko**: A library used to handle SSH connections, which is especially useful when working with network devices.

- Install Paramiko by running:

```bash

pip install paramiko
```

o **Requests**: A simple library for making HTTP requests, commonly used when interacting with APIs.

- Install Requests by running:

```bash

pip install requests
```

After installing these packages, you'll be ready to begin automating network management tasks.

Overview of IDEs and Tools for Network Automation

An Integrated Development Environment (IDE) is a software application that provides tools for writing, testing, and debugging code. When it comes to network automation, choosing the right IDE can greatly improve productivity. Below are some popular IDEs and tools commonly used in network automation:

1. **VS Code (Visual Studio Code):**
   o **Why Use It?**: VS Code is lightweight, fast, and highly customizable. It supports Python out of the box and has a vast collection of extensions that help with debugging, linting, and version control.
   o **Features**:
     ▪ Syntax highlighting and IntelliSense (auto-completion)
     ▪ Integrated terminal
     ▪ Debugging tools
     ▪ Git integration
     ▪ Python extensions for linting and testing
   o **How to Set It Up**:

32

- Install VS Code from here.
- Install the Python extension by searching for "Python" in the Extensions Marketplace within VS Code.

2. **PyCharm:**
   - **Why Use It?**: PyCharm is a full-fledged IDE specifically designed for Python development. It comes with several advanced features, such as automatic code completion, real-time error checking, and integrated testing support.
   - **Features**:
     - Code refactoring tools
     - Built-in debugger
     - Python-specific libraries pre-configured
     - Easy integration with virtual environments
   - **How to Set It Up**:
     - Download and install PyCharm from here.
     - The community edition is free, while the professional version offers additional features.

3. **Jupyter Notebook:**
   - **Why Use It?**: Jupyter Notebooks are great for interactive development, especially when testing small snippets of code. It is commonly used for

data analysis and automation tasks, allowing you to combine code, results, and documentation in one document.

- o **Features**:
  - Interactive coding environment
  - Supports Python and many other languages
  - Easy to share with others
- o **How to Set It Up**:
  - Install Jupyter by running:

```bash
pip install notebook
```

  - Start Jupyter by typing:

```bash
jupyter notebook
```

4. **Text Editors (Sublime Text, Atom):**
   - o **Why Use Them?**: If you're looking for a lightweight solution, text editors like Sublime Text or Atom are great choices. While they lack the features of full-fledged IDEs, they are quick to set up and offer sufficient tools for small-scale network automation scripts.

34

- o **Features**:
  - Syntax highlighting
  - Fast and responsive
  - Highly extensible with plugins
- o **How to Set It Up**:
  - Download and install Sublime Text from here.
  - Download and install Atom from here.

Configuring the Environment for Automation Scripts

Once you have Python and your IDE installed, the next step is configuring the environment for writing network automation scripts. Here's how you can set it up:

1. **Setting Up a Virtual Environment:**
   - o Using a virtual environment helps isolate project dependencies, ensuring that libraries installed for one project don't interfere with others.
   - o To set up a virtual environment:
     - **Step 1**: Install `virtualenv`:

       ```bash

       pip install virtualenv
       ```

- **Step 2**: Create a virtual environment in your project directory:

```bash
```

```
virtualenv myenv
```

- **Step 3**: Activate the virtual environment:
    - On Windows:

    ```bash
    ```

    ```
    myenv\Scripts\activate
    ```

    - On macOS/Linux:

    ```bash
    ```

    ```
    source
    myenv/bin/activate
    ```

- **Step 4**: Install required libraries (e.g., Netmiko, NAPALM) inside the virtual environment using `pip`.

2. **Organizing Scripts and Files:**
    o Create a structured directory for your scripts. A typical directory might look like:

    ```bash
    ```

```
/my_project
├── /scripts
│      ├── config_backup.py
│      ├── device_configuration.py
├── /logs
├── /config
├── requirements.txt
└── README.md
```

- o The `scripts` folder will contain your Python automation scripts, while `logs` is where you can store output files and logs. The `config` folder can hold configuration files, and `requirements.txt` lists all the libraries your project depends on.

3. **Version Control with Git:**

   - o It's a good practice to use **Git** for version control, especially for larger projects. This allows you to keep track of code changes and collaborate with others.
   - o Install **Git** from here.
   - o Initialize a Git repository in your project folder:

```
bash
```

```
git init
```

o You can then commit your code and push it to a GitHub or GitLab repository.

4. Testing Your Setup:

o After setting up the environment, write a simple script to test your configuration. For example, a script that connects to a network device using **Netmiko** to retrieve information:

```python
from netmiko import ConnectHandler

device = {
    'device_type': 'cisco_ios',
    'host': '192.168.1.1',
    'username': 'admin',
    'password': 'password',
}

net_connect                         =
ConnectHandler(**device)
output                              =
net_connect.send_command('show
version')
print(output)
```

o Running this script will verify that your environment is correctly set up and capable of communicating with network devices.

This chapter provides you with all the foundational tools you need to begin writing automation scripts for network management. With Python installed and your IDE configured, you're now ready to dive into creating more sophisticated network automation workflows. In the next chapter, we will explore some key libraries and tools that can help automate network configurations, monitoring, and more.

CHAPTER 4

PYTHON BASICS FOR NETWORKING

Python Syntax Essentials for Beginners

Before diving into network automation with Python, it's important to grasp the basics of Python syntax. These fundamentals will provide a solid foundation for writing scripts that can automate network tasks. Let's cover the essential elements of Python that every beginner should understand.

1. **Variables and Data Types:** Python supports several built-in data types such as integers, floats, strings, and booleans. Variables in Python are dynamically typed, meaning you don't need to declare their type explicitly.

    o **Example:**

    ```python
    python

    ip_address = "192.168.1.1"   # String
    ```

```
subnet_mask   =   "255.255.255.0"   #
String
port = 22                           #
Integer
is_active = True                    #
Boolean
```

2. **Lists:** Lists are used to store multiple items in a single variable. They are ordered and mutable, allowing you to change, add, or remove elements.

   o **Example:**

   ```python
   python
   ```

   ```python
   network_devices    =     ["Router",
   "Switch", "Firewall"]
   network_devices.append("Access
   Point")  # Add item
   print(network_devices[0])  # Output:
   Router
   ```

3. **Loops:** Loops are used to repeat a block of code multiple times. There are two primary types in Python: `for` loops and `while` loops.

   o **For Loop Example:**

   ```python
   python
   ```

```
for device in network_devices:
    print(device)        #    Outputs:
Router,    Switch,    Firewall,    Access
Point
```

- o **While Loop Example:**

```python

count = 0
while count < 3:
    print("Connecting to device...")
    count += 1
```

4. **Conditional Statements:** Conditional statements allow you to execute certain blocks of code based on specific conditions.

- o **Example:**

```python

if is_active:
    print("Device is active")
else:
    print("Device is inactive")
```

5. **Functions:** Functions are used to encapsulate code into reusable blocks. Functions can accept arguments and return values.

42

o **Example:**

```python
def ping_device(ip):
    print(f"Pinging {ip}")
ping_device("192.168.1.1")
```

6. **Dictionaries:** Dictionaries allow you to store data as key-value pairs. They are ideal for mapping information, such as IP addresses to device names.

o **Example:**

```python
devices = {"Router": "192.168.1.1",
"Switch": "192.168.1.2"}
print(devices["Router"])    # Output:
192.168.1.1
```

These syntax essentials will form the backbone of your network automation scripts, allowing you to work with devices, process data, and implement network management logic.

Introduction to Libraries Useful for Network Automation

Python has a rich ecosystem of libraries designed for network automation. Here are some of the most useful libraries when working with network devices:

1. **Netmiko:**

   o **Netmiko** is one of the most popular libraries for network automation. It simplifies the process of connecting to network devices via SSH and sending commands. Netmiko supports multiple device types, including Cisco, Juniper, and Arista.

   o **Installation:**

   bash

   ```
   pip install netmiko
   ```

   o **Usage:** Netmiko allows you to automate network configurations, collect data, and perform tests on devices like routers, switches, and firewalls.

   python

   ```
   from netmiko import ConnectHandler
   ```

44

```
device = {
    'device_type': 'cisco_ios',
    'host': '192.168.1.1',
    'username': 'admin',
    'password': 'password',
}

net_connect               =
ConnectHandler(**device)
output                    =
net_connect.send_command('show
version')
print(output)
```

2. **Paramiko:**

   o **Paramiko** is another widely used library for handling SSH connections. Unlike Netmiko, Paramiko is more low-level, giving you more control over SSH sessions and file transfers (SFTP). It is useful for situations where you need fine-grained control over the connection process.

   o **Installation:**

   ```bash
   ```

   ```
   pip install paramiko
   ```

45

- o **Usage:**

```python
python

import paramiko

ssh = paramiko.SSHClient()
ssh.set_missing_host_key_policy(par
amiko.AutoAddPolicy())
ssh.connect('192.168.1.1',
username='admin',
password='password')

stdin,      stdout,      stderr      =
ssh.exec_command('show version')
print(stdout.read().decode())
ssh.close()
```

3. **PyShark:**

- o **PyShark** is a wrapper around the popular packet analysis tool Wireshark. It allows you to capture and analyze network traffic using Python. This library is particularly useful for automating network analysis tasks and extracting meaningful data from packet captures.
- o **Installation:**

```bash
bash
```

```
pip install pyshark
```

o **Usage:**

```python
python
```

```
import pyshark
```

```
capture                                    =
pyshark.FileCapture('example.pcap')
for packet in capture:
    print(packet)
```

4. **NAPALM (Network Automation and Programmability Abstraction Layer with Multivendor support):**

   o **NAPALM** is a powerful library that abstracts the complexity of network automation by providing a uniform API for managing network devices across multiple vendors. It supports devices from Cisco, Juniper, Arista, and more.

   o **Installation:**

```bash
bash
```

```
pip install napalm
```

- o **Usage:**

```
python

from              napalm              import
get_network_driver

driver = get_network_driver('ios')
device    =    driver('192.168.1.1',
'admin', 'password')
device.open()
print(device.get_facts())
device.close()
```

These libraries are just a few examples of the tools that make Python a powerful language for network automation. They allow you to interact with network devices, automate configurations, and perform real-time network analysis with ease.

Basic Scripting Examples to Interact with Network Devices

Now that you are familiar with Python syntax and essential libraries, let's look at a few simple scripting examples to interact with network devices. These examples will help you understand how to use Python to automate tasks like connecting to devices, collecting information, and making changes.

1. **Connecting to a Cisco Device and Fetching Information:**

```python
python

from netmiko import ConnectHandler

# Device details
device = {
    'device_type': 'cisco_ios',
    'host': '192.168.1.1',
    'username': 'admin',
    'password': 'password',
}

# Connect to the device
net_connect = ConnectHandler(**device)

# Send a command to retrieve information
about the device
output = net_connect.send_command('show ip
interface brief')
print(output)

# Close the connection
```

```
net_connect.disconnect()
```

2. Automating Configuration Changes:

If you need to automate the process of configuring multiple devices, you can use Python to loop through a list of devices and push the same configuration.

```python
from netmiko import ConnectHandler

devices = [
    {'device_type': 'cisco_ios', 'host':
'192.168.1.1', 'username': 'admin',
'password': 'password'},
    {'device_type': 'cisco_ios', 'host':
'192.168.1.2', 'username': 'admin',
'password': 'password'},
]

for device in devices:
    net_connect = ConnectHandler(**device)
    config_commands = [
        'hostname NewRouterName',
        'interface GigabitEthernet0/1',
        'ip address 192.168.2.1
255.255.255.0',
        'no shutdown'
```

```
]
```

```
net_connect.send_config_set(config_comman
ds)
    print(f"Configuration    applied    to
{device['host']}")
    net_connect.disconnect()
```

3. Collecting Data from Multiple Devices:

This script connects to several devices, collects their uptime, and stores the results in a dictionary.

```python
from netmiko import ConnectHandler

devices = [
    {'device_type': 'cisco_ios', 'host':
'192.168.1.1',    'username':    'admin',
'password': 'password'},
    {'device_type': 'cisco_ios', 'host':
'192.168.1.2',    'username':    'admin',
'password': 'password'},
]

uptime_info = {}

for device in devices:
```

```
    net_connect = ConnectHandler(**device)
    uptime                              =
net_connect.send_command('show  version  |
include uptime')
        uptime_info[device['host']] = uptime
        net_connect.disconnect()

print(uptime_info)
```

This chapter provided you with the essential Python syntax for beginners, along with introductions to important libraries used for network automation. With these tools, you can begin automating tasks such as retrieving information from devices, applying configurations, and collecting network statistics. In the next chapter, we will explore how to handle network device configurations in greater detail and dive deeper into practical network automation examples.

CHAPTER 5

INTERACTING WITH NETWORK DEVICES USING SSH

Connecting to Network Devices via SSH Using Python

SSH (Secure Shell) is one of the most common and secure methods for remotely connecting to network devices such as routers, switches, and firewalls. Python, with the help of libraries like **Netmiko** and **Paramiko**, allows you to automate these SSH connections, simplifying network management tasks.

1. **Using Netmiko for SSH Connections:**

   Netmiko simplifies working with network devices via SSH. It abstracts the details of the connection process and provides a straightforward API for interacting with devices.

   o **Installation:** If you haven't already installed **Netmiko**, use the following command:

```bash
bash
```

```
pip install netmiko
```

o **Basic SSH Connection with Netmiko:**
   Here's an example of how to establish an SSH
   connection to a Cisco device and send a
   command:

```python
python

from netmiko import ConnectHandler

# Define device details
device = {
    'device_type': 'cisco_ios',
    'host': '192.168.1.1',          #
Device IP address
    'username': 'admin',            #
Device login username
    'password': 'password',         #
Device login password
    'secret': 'secret',             #
Enable password (if needed)
}

# Establish SSH connection
net_connect                         =
ConnectHandler(**device)
```

54

```
# Enter enable mode (if required)
net_connect.enable()

# Send command to the device
output                           =
net_connect.send_command('show    ip
interface brief')

# Print the output
print(output)

# Close the SSH session
net_connect.disconnect()
```

In this example:

- **device_type** specifies the type of device (in this case, a Cisco router).
- **host, username,** and **password** are used to authenticate.
- **secret** is used to enter enable mode if required for privileged commands.
- **send_command()** sends the command to the device and returns the output.

o **Using SSH with Other Devices:** Netmiko supports many types of network devices (e.g., Juniper, Arista, HP). You can change the `device_type` to match the device you're connecting to.

Automating Device Configuration with Python Scripts

Automating device configurations is one of the primary use cases for Python in network automation. Using SSH and Python scripts, you can push configuration changes across multiple devices, ensuring consistency and reducing human error.

1. **Automating Configuration Changes:**

   Here's an example of how to automate basic configuration tasks like changing the hostname and interface IP address of a Cisco device:

```python
python

from netmiko import ConnectHandler

# Define device details
device = {
    'device_type': 'cisco_ios',
    'host': '192.168.1.1',
    'username': 'admin',
```

```
    'password': 'password',
    'secret': 'secret',
}

# Establish SSH connection
net_connect = ConnectHandler(**device)

# Enter enable mode
net_connect.enable()

# Define configuration commands
config_commands = [
    'hostname NewRouterName',
    'interface GigabitEthernet0/1',
    'ip         address         192.168.2.1
255.255.255.0',
    'no shutdown',
]

# Send configuration commands to the device
output                                    =
net_connect.send_config_set(config_comman
ds)

# Print the output
print(output)

# Save configuration to the device
net_connect.save_config()
```

57

```
# Close the connection
net_connect.disconnect()
```

In this example:

- o **send_config_set()** sends a list of configuration commands to the device.
- o After sending the configuration commands, we use **save_config()** to save the changes to the device's configuration.

2. **Applying Configurations to Multiple Devices:**

If you need to apply configurations to multiple devices, you can loop through a list of devices and apply the same commands to each one. Here's how you can do that:

```python

from netmiko import ConnectHandler

# List of devices
devices = [
    {'device_type': 'cisco_ios', 'host':
'192.168.1.1', 'username': 'admin',
'password': 'password', 'secret':
'secret'},
```

```
    {'device_type': 'cisco_ios', 'host':
'192.168.1.2', 'username': 'admin',
'password': 'password', 'secret':
'secret'}
]


# Configuration commands to apply
config_commands = [
    'hostname NewRouterName',
    'interface GigabitEthernet0/1',
    'ip        address        192.168.2.1
255.255.255.0',
    'no shutdown',
]


for device in devices:
    # Establish SSH connection
    net_connect = ConnectHandler(**device)

    # Enter enable mode
    net_connect.enable()

    # Send configuration commands to the
device
    output                             =
net_connect.send_config_set(config_comman
ds)
    print(f"Configuration applied to
{device['host']}")
```

```
# Save configuration
net_connect.save_config()

# Close the connection
net_connect.disconnect()
```

This script connects to two devices in a loop and applies the same configuration commands. This approach allows you to scale your automation efforts by easily applying changes to multiple devices at once.

Error Handling and Debugging Scripts

When automating network tasks, it's crucial to implement proper error handling to ensure your scripts run smoothly and can recover from unexpected issues. Here are some common error-handling techniques for working with network automation scripts:

1. **Handling Connection Failures:**

   Sometimes, SSH connections might fail due to network issues or incorrect credentials. Using **try-**

except blocks, you can gracefully handle these situations.

python

```
from netmiko import ConnectHandler
from       netmiko.ssh_exception       import
NetMikoTimeoutException,
NetMikoAuthenticationException

device = {
    'device_type': 'cisco_ios',
    'host': '192.168.1.1',
    'username': 'admin',
    'password': 'password',
    'secret': 'secret',
}

try:
    # Establish SSH connection
    net_connect = ConnectHandler(**device)
    net_connect.enable()
    print("Connection successful!")
except NetMikoTimeoutException:
    print(f"Connection to {device['host']}
timed out.")
except NetMikoAuthenticationException:
    print(f"Authentication    failed    for
{device['host']}.")
```

```
except Exception as e:
    print(f"An error occurred: {e}")
```

- o **NetMikoTimeoutException** handles cases where the device is unreachable.
- o **NetMikoAuthenticationException** catches authentication failures.
- o The generic **Exception** block catches any other unforeseen errors.

2. Debugging with Logging:

To diagnose issues with your scripts, it's helpful to enable logging to capture details about script execution. Python's built-in **logging** module can be used to log events, warnings, and errors.

```python
import logging
from netmiko import ConnectHandler

# Set up logging
logging.basicConfig(filename='network_aut
omation.log', level=logging.DEBUG)

device = {
    'device_type': 'cisco_ios',
    'host': '192.168.1.1',
```

```
        'username': 'admin',
        'password': 'password',
        'secret': 'secret',
}

try:
    # Establish SSH connection
    net_connect = ConnectHandler(**device)
    net_connect.enable()
    logging.info(f"Successfully connected
to {device['host']}")
except Exception as e:
    logging.error(f"Error connecting to
{device['host']}: {e}")
    print(f"Error connecting to
{device['host']}")
```

The logging module allows you to capture successful connections, errors, and other important details. This is especially useful for tracking script execution over time and troubleshooting issues.

3. **Debugging Output:**

When troubleshooting a script, it's helpful to print or log intermediate outputs. For example, you can print the output of commands you send to devices to ensure that you're receiving the expected responses:

```python
python

output = net_connect.send_command('show ip
interface brief')
print("Command Output:")
print(output)
```

By reviewing this output, you can identify if the correct command was executed and whether the device returned the expected information.

This chapter introduced you to SSH-based network automation using Python, specifically with **Netmiko**. We covered how to establish SSH connections, automate configuration changes across multiple devices, and implement error handling and debugging techniques to ensure your scripts run smoothly. In the next chapter, we'll explore more advanced network automation scenarios, including integrating with network monitoring systems and APIs.

CHAPTER 6

WORKING WITH SNMP FOR NETWORK MANAGEMENT

Introduction to SNMP (Simple Network Management Protocol)

SNMP (Simple Network Management Protocol) is one of the most widely used protocols for managing and monitoring network devices such as routers, switches, servers, and printers. It allows network administrators to gather and manage information about network performance, usage, and faults. SNMP operates in a client-server model where devices (servers) are referred to as **agents**, and the network management software or systems querying the devices are known as the **manager**.

SNMP works by exchanging messages called **protocol data units (PDUs)** between the manager and agent. It uses three primary components:

1. **SNMP Manager**: The system that queries and receives data from SNMP agents, typically a network management system (NMS).

2. **SNMP Agent**: Software running on network devices (routers, switches, etc.) that responds to requests from the SNMP manager.

3. **MIB (Management Information Base)**: A database that defines the structure of the data available from the SNMP agent. The MIB stores objects that represent the attributes of a device, such as its CPU utilization or memory usage.

SNMP operates on three versions:

- **SNMPv1**: The original version, providing basic features with minimal security.
- **SNMPv2c**: Enhanced version with better performance but still uses community-based authentication.
- **SNMPv3**: The most secure version, offering encryption and authentication for better security.

SNMP is invaluable for network automation because it allows network administrators to query network devices for important statistics, monitor network health, and even make configuration changes remotely.

Using Python to Query Network Devices via SNMP

Python provides a convenient way to interact with SNMP-enabled devices using the **PySNMP** library. PySNMP allows you to query and manipulate SNMP devices programmatically.

1. **Installing PySNMP:** To get started with SNMP in Python, you need to install the **PySNMP** library. You can install it via **pip**:

```bash
bash
```

```bash
pip install pysnmp
```

2. **Basic SNMP Get Request:** The **SNMP GET** request is used to retrieve information from a network device. Here's a simple example of how to use PySNMP to perform an SNMP GET request to query a device for its system description.

```python
python
```

```python
from pysnmp.hlapi import *

# SNMP device details
ip_address = '192.168.1.1'
```

```python
community = 'public'  # SNMP community
string (read-only access)
oid = '1.3.6.1.2.1.1.1.0'  # OID for system
description

# Perform SNMP GET request
iterator = getCmd(SnmpEngine(),

CommunityData(community),

UdpTransportTarget((ip_address, 161)),
                ContextData(),

ObjectType(ObjectIdentity(oid)))

# Process the result
error_indication,           error_status,
error_index, var_binds = next(iterator)

if error_indication:
    print(f"Error: {error_indication}")
elif error_status:
    print(f"Error                   Status:
{error_status.prettyPrint()}")
else:
    for var_bind in var_binds:
        print(f"Result: {var_bind}")
```

In this example:

- o **getCmd()** is used to send an SNMP GET request.
- o The **OID (Object Identifier)** for the **system description** (1.3.6.1.2.1.1.1.0) is queried, which returns basic information about the device.
- o The response is printed if the query is successful.

Note: You must have the correct community string (e.g., 'public' or 'private') for authentication.

3. **SNMP Walk:** To query a device for multiple SNMP values, the **SNMP WALK** operation is used. It retrieves all values associated with a particular OID or subtree.

Here's how to perform an SNMP WALK to retrieve multiple system parameters (e.g., CPU load, memory utilization):

```python

from pysnmp.hlapi import *

ip_address = '192.168.1.1'
community = 'public'
oid_base = '1.3.6.1.2.1.2.2.1'   # OID for
interface statistics
```

```
# Perform SNMP WALK
iterator = nextCmd(SnmpEngine(),

CommunityData(community),

UdpTransportTarget((ip_address, 161)),
                ContextData(),

ObjectType(ObjectIdentity(oid_base)))

# Process the result
for    error_indication,    error_status,
error_index, var_binds in iterator:
    if error_indication:
        print(f"Error:
{error_indication}")
    elif error_status:
        print(f"Error              Status:
{error_status.prettyPrint()}")
    else:
        for var_bind in var_binds:
            print(f"Result: {var_bind}")
```

In this example:

- o **nextCmd()** is used to perform the SNMP
  WALK operation.

o   We use an OID (1.3.6.1.2.1.2.2.1) that covers various interface statistics (e.g., interface status, packet count).

4. **SNMP Set (Configuration Change):** SNMP also allows for **SET** operations, where you can configure devices remotely. Here's how to change the system description of a device using SNMP SET:

```python
from pysnmp.hlapi import *

ip_address = '192.168.1.1'
community = 'private'  # SNMP community string (write access)
oid = '1.3.6.1.2.1.1.1.0' # OID for system description
new_value = 'New system description'

# Perform SNMP SET request
iterator = setCmd(SnmpEngine(),

CommunityData(community),

UdpTransportTarget((ip_address, 161)),
            ContextData(),
```

```
ObjectType(ObjectIdentity(oid),
new_value))

# Process the result
error_indication,            error_status,
error_index, var_binds = next(iterator)

if error_indication:
    print(f"Error: {error_indication}")
elif error_status:
    print(f"Error            Status:
{error_status.prettyPrint()}")
else:
    print(f"Successfully set new value:
{new_value}")
```

This script sets a new value for the system description on the device specified by the OID.

Real-World Examples of SNMP Automation for Monitoring Network Devices

1. **Monitoring Device Uptime:** SNMP is frequently used to monitor the uptime of network devices. By querying the **sysUpTime** OID (1.3.6.1.2.1.1.3.0), you can track how long a

device has been running without a reboot. Here's an example:

```python
from pysnmp.hlapi import *

ip_address = '192.168.1.1'
community = 'public'
uptime_oid   =   '1.3.6.1.2.1.1.3.0'      #
sysUpTime OID

# Perform SNMP GET request for uptime
iterator = getCmd(SnmpEngine(),

CommunityData(community),

UdpTransportTarget((ip_address, 161)),
                ContextData(),

ObjectType(ObjectIdentity(uptime_oid)))

# Process the result
error_indication,               error_status,
error_index, var_binds = next(iterator)

if error_indication:
    print(f"Error: {error_indication}")
elif error_status:
```

```
    print(f"Error                Status:
{error_status.prettyPrint()}")
else:
    for var_bind in var_binds:
        print(f"Device              uptime:
{var_bind}")
```

This script allows you to retrieve the system uptime and monitor whether the device has experienced any unexpected reboots.

2. **Network Interface Monitoring:** You can use SNMP to monitor network interfaces for traffic, errors, or status. By querying interfaces using the **IF-MIB** OID (1.3.6.1.2.1.2.2), you can track traffic on specific interfaces.

```
python

from pysnmp.hlapi import *

ip_address = '192.168.1.1'
community = 'public'
interface_oid = '1.3.6.1.2.1.2.2.1.10'   #
OID for incoming traffic (bytes)

# Perform SNMP GET request for interface
traffic
```

```
iterator = getCmd(SnmpEngine(),

CommunityData(community),

UdpTransportTarget((ip_address, 161)),
                ContextData(),

ObjectType(ObjectIdentity(interface_oid))
)

# Process the result
error_indication,              error_status,
error_index, var_binds = next(iterator)

if error_indication:
    print(f"Error: {error_indication}")
elif error_status:
    print(f"Error              Status:
{error_status.prettyPrint()}")
else:
    for var_bind in var_binds:
        print(f"Interface      traffic:
{var_bind}")
```

This script retrieves the number of bytes received on a particular network interface, allowing you to monitor traffic usage and spot potential network congestion.

In this chapter, we've introduced SNMP and shown how Python can interact with SNMP-enabled devices to collect and manage network data. By using libraries like **PySNMP**, network administrators can automate monitoring tasks, retrieve important device information, and even make configuration changes. The examples provided give you the foundation to build robust SNMP-based automation for monitoring network health in real-world environments.

CHAPTER 7

AUTOMATING NETWORK CONFIGURATION CHANGES

Writing Python Scripts to Make Bulk Configuration Changes

When managing multiple network devices, applying configuration changes manually can be time-consuming and error-prone. Automating network configuration changes using Python can drastically improve efficiency, reduce human error, and ensure consistency across your network devices.

1. **Bulk Configuration with Python:** Python allows you to apply configuration changes to multiple devices simultaneously using loops and configuration templates. The **Netmiko** library, for example, provides a way to connect to devices via SSH and execute commands on them programmatically.

Here's a simple example where Python is used to apply the same configuration to multiple Cisco routers:

```python
from netmiko import ConnectHandler

# List of devices to configure
devices = [
    {'device_type': 'cisco_ios', 'host':
'192.168.1.1', 'username': 'admin',
'password': 'password', 'secret':
'secret'},
    {'device_type': 'cisco_ios', 'host':
'192.168.1.2', 'username': 'admin',
'password': 'password', 'secret':
'secret'},
]

# Configuration commands to apply
config_commands = [
    'hostname NewRouter',
    'interface GigabitEthernet0/1',
    'ip        address        192.168.2.1
255.255.255.0',
    'no shutdown',
    'router ospf 1',
```

```
    'network  192.168.2.0  0.0.0.255   area
0',
]


# Loop through each device and apply the
configuration
for device in devices:
    try:
        # Establish SSH connection
        net_connect                       =
ConnectHandler(**device)
        net_connect.enable()

        # Apply configuration commands
        output                            =
net_connect.send_config_set(config_comman
ds)
        print(f"Configuration  applied   to
{device['host']}")

        # Save configuration to the device
        net_connect.save_config()

        # Disconnect after configuration
        net_connect.disconnect()
    except Exception as e:
        print(f"Failed    to    configure
{device['host']}: {e}")
```

79

- o **send_config_set()**: Sends a list of configuration commands to the device.
- o **save_config()**: Saves the configuration to the device.
- o The script iterates over a list of devices, applying the same configuration set to each one.

This example demonstrates how to apply configurations to multiple devices with minimal effort.

2. **Using Variables for Dynamic Configurations:** Python scripts can also make configuration changes dynamic by using variables to tailor commands for each device. For example, if you have different IP addresses for each router, you can customize the configuration based on the device's IP address:

```python

from netmiko import ConnectHandler

# Device-specific configurations
devices = [
    {'device_type': 'cisco_ios', 'host':
'192.168.1.1',    'username':    'admin',
```

80

```
'password':       'password',       'secret':
'secret', 'ip_address': '192.168.1.1'},
    {'device_type':  'cisco_ios',  'host':
'192.168.1.2',      'username':      'admin',
'password':       'password',       'secret':
'secret', 'ip_address': '192.168.1.2'},
]


for device in devices:
    try:
        # Establish SSH connection
        net_connect                         =
ConnectHandler(**device)
        net_connect.enable()


        # Dynamic configuration command
        config_commands = [
            f'hostname             Router-
{device["ip_address"]}',
            f'interface
GigabitEthernet0/1',
            f'ip                   address
{device["ip_address"]} 255.255.255.0',
            'no shutdown',
        ]


        # Send configuration commands
```

```
        output                        =
net_connect.send_config_set(config_comman
ds)
        print(f"Configuration applied to
{device['host']}")

        # Save configuration
        net_connect.save_config()

        # Disconnect
        net_connect.disconnect()
    except Exception as e:
        print(f"Failed    to    configure
{device['host']}: {e}")
```

- o Here, **device["ip_address"]** is used as a dynamic variable in the configuration commands to set different IP addresses for each device.
- o This approach allows you to tailor configuration changes to specific device attributes.

Applying Configuration Changes to Routers, Switches, and Firewalls

The process for applying configuration changes is largely the same across different types of network devices such as routers, switches, and firewalls, but the commands may differ based on the device type. Let's look at examples for each device:

1. **Configuring Cisco Routers:** Cisco routers use **IOS** (Internetwork Operating System), and you can apply configurations for interfaces, routing protocols, and security settings. A typical configuration might involve setting up interfaces and routing protocols like OSPF or EIGRP:

```python
config_commands = [
    'hostname Router1',
    'interface GigabitEthernet0/1',
    'ip         address         192.168.1.1
255.255.255.0',
    'no shutdown',
    'router ospf 1',
    'network 192.168.1.0 0.0.0.255 area
0',
]
```

2. **Configuring Cisco Switches:** Cisco switches often require VLAN configurations and port assignments. For example:

```python
```

```
config_commands = [
    'hostname Switch1',
    'vlan 10',
    'name Sales',
    'interface range GigabitEthernet0/1 -
24',
    'switchport mode access',
    'switchport access vlan 10',
]
```

3. **Configuring Firewalls (e.g., Cisco ASA):** Firewalls may require security policy configurations such as access control lists (ACLs), NAT (Network Address Translation), and VPN settings. An example command to configure an ASA firewall could look like this:

```
python
```

```
config_commands = [
    'hostname ASA1',
    'interface GigabitEthernet0/1',
    'nameif outside',
    'security-level 0',
    'ip          address          203.0.113.1
255.255.255.0',
    'no shutdown',
```

```
'object network obj_any',
'subnet 0.0.0.0 255.255.255.255',
'nat       (inside,outside)       dynamic
interface',
]
```

  o Each of these configurations is tailored for the specific type of device (router, switch, firewall), but the process of applying them with Python remains consistent.

Using Templates and Version Control for Configurations

1. **Configuration Templates:**

Templates can help standardize configurations across multiple devices. Instead of writing configuration commands directly into your Python scripts, you can create configuration templates and fill in the variables dynamically. This can be done using **Python's string formatting** or a **template engine** like **Jinja2**.

Example using Python string formatting:

```python
```

```
template = """
hostname {hostname}
interface {interface}
ip address {ip_address} 255.255.255.0
no shutdown
"""
```

```
config                                    =
template.format(hostname='Router1',
interface='GigabitEthernet0/1',
ip_address='192.168.1.1')
print(config)
```

Using Jinja2 for More Complex Templates:

```
python
```

```
from jinja2 import Template
```

```
template = """
hostname {{ hostname }}
interface {{ interface }}
ip address {{ ip_address }} 255.255.255.0
no shutdown
"""
```

```
jinja_template = Template(template)
config                                    =
jinja_template.render(hostname='Router1',
```

```
interface='GigabitEthernet0/1',
ip_address='192.168.1.1')
print(config)
```

o **Jinja2** provides more flexibility and features for generating configuration files dynamically.

2. **Version Control for Configurations:**

Using **Git** for version control of your configuration files ensures that you can track changes, roll back to previous versions, and collaborate with others effectively. Here's a simple workflow:

o Initialize a Git repository in your configuration directory:

```
bash
```

```
git init
```

o Add and commit changes to your configuration files:

```
bash
```

```
git add router_config.txt
git commit -m "Initial configuration
for Router1"
```

87

o Push the configuration files to a remote repository (e.g., GitHub or GitLab):

```
bash

git remote add origin <your-repo-
url>
git push -u origin master
```

Version control allows you to track who made specific changes to configurations and when, making it easier to manage configuration updates across your network devices.

In this chapter, we've learned how to automate network configuration changes using Python. We discussed bulk configuration changes across multiple devices, how to apply these changes to routers, switches, and firewalls, and the importance of using templates and version control to manage configurations effectively. With these tools, you can significantly improve the efficiency, consistency, and reliability of network management tasks. In the next chapter, we will explore monitoring network performance and health using Python.

CHAPTER 8

MONITORING NETWORK HEALTH

Automating Network Performance Monitoring

Network performance monitoring is essential for ensuring that your network is running smoothly and efficiently. It involves tracking various metrics such as bandwidth usage, latency, and packet loss, which can help identify bottlenecks, potential failures, or security issues in the network. By automating network monitoring, you can continuously collect data, set thresholds, and receive alerts without the need for manual intervention.

1. **Using SNMP for Performance Monitoring: SNMP (Simple Network Management Protocol)** is one of the most popular protocols for monitoring network health. It allows you to gather valuable performance metrics like interface statistics, CPU utilization, memory usage, and more from network devices such as routers and switches.

Python's **PySNMP** library can be used to automate the process of retrieving performance data from SNMP-enabled devices. Here's how to query for network interface statistics (e.g., bandwidth usage) using SNMP.

```python
python

from pysnmp.hlapi import *

ip_address = '192.168.1.1'
community = 'public'
if_in_octets_oid = '1.3.6.1.2.1.2.2.1.10'
# OID for incoming traffic (bytes)
if_out_octets_oid = '1.3.6.1.2.1.2.2.1.16'
# OID for outgoing traffic (bytes)

# Perform SNMP GET request for incoming and
outgoing traffic
iterator = getCmd(SnmpEngine(),

CommunityData(community),

UdpTransportTarget((ip_address, 161)),
                ContextData(),

ObjectType(ObjectIdentity(if_in_octets_oi
d)),
```

91

```
ObjectType(ObjectIdentity(if_out_octets_o
id)))

# Process the result
error_indication,            error_status,
error_index, var_binds = next(iterator)

if error_indication:
    print(f"Error: {error_indication}")
elif error_status:
    print(f"Error              Status:
{error_status.prettyPrint()}")
else:
    for var_bind in var_binds:
        print(f"Traffic Data: {var_bind}")
```

In this example:

- o **if_in_octets_oid** and **if_out_octets_oid** are SNMP OIDs that correspond to incoming and outgoing traffic statistics.
- o This script retrieves and prints the bytes received and transmitted over an interface, which can then be used to monitor bandwidth usage in real time.

2. **Automating Polling and Alerts:** For continuous monitoring, you can set up automated polling of

92

devices at regular intervals. Using Python's `time.sleep()` function, you can create a loop that queries network devices every few seconds or minutes. Additionally, you can implement alerting when performance thresholds (such as high bandwidth usage or packet loss) are exceeded.

```python
import time
from pysnmp.hlapi import *

def           monitor_network(ip_address,
community):
    while True:
        # SNMP request to get interface
traffic (example)
        iterator = getCmd(SnmpEngine(),

CommunityData(community),

UdpTransportTarget((ip_address, 161)),
                        ContextData(),

ObjectType(ObjectIdentity('1.3.6.1.2.1.2.
2.1.10')))  # Incoming traffic
```

93

```
        error_indication,    error_status,
error_index, var_binds = next(iterator)

        if error_indication:
            print(f"Error:
{error_indication}")
        elif error_status:
            print(f"Error        Status:
{error_status.prettyPrint()}")
        else:
            for var_bind in var_binds:
                traffic_data = var_bind[1]
                print(f"Incoming   traffic:
{traffic_data}")
                if    traffic_data    >
10000000:  # Example threshold (10 MB)
                    print("Alert:    High
traffic detected!")

        time.sleep(60)    # Delay  for  60
seconds before checking again

monitor_network('192.168.1.1', 'public')
```

- o **time.sleep(60)**: Pauses the script for 60 seconds between each query, enabling continuous monitoring.
- o The script checks incoming traffic and triggers an alert if it exceeds a threshold.

Using Python for Real-Time Network Health Checks

In addition to SNMP, Python can be used for other real-time network health checks, such as monitoring ping latency and packet loss, which are often the first indicators of network problems.

1. **Using Ping for Latency and Packet Loss Monitoring:**

   Python's `subprocess` module allows you to execute system commands, such as **ping**, directly from your Python script. This is an effective way to monitor network latency and packet loss in real-time.

   Here's a simple script that uses **ping** to check the latency and packet loss to a network device:

```python
python

import subprocess
import time

def ping_device(ip_address):
    # Execute the ping command
```

```
    result = subprocess.run(['ping', '-c',
'4', ip_address], stdout=subprocess.PIPE,
stderr=subprocess.PIPE)

    if result.returncode == 0:
        # If ping was successful
        output                         =
result.stdout.decode('utf-8')
        print(f"Ping    to    {ip_address}
successful!")
        print(output)
    else:
        print(f"Failed      to      ping
{ip_address}")

def monitor_latency(ip_address):
    while True:
        print(f"Pinging  {ip_address}  to
check latency...")
        ping_device(ip_address)
        time.sleep(60)   # Delay for 60
seconds before checking again

monitor_latency('192.168.1.1')
```

- o **subprocess.run()** runs the ping command and collects the output.
- o The script pings the target device (192.168.1.1 in this example) and checks for packet loss and

latency. It will then print the results to the console.

o The script continues to ping the device every minute.

2. **Parsing Ping Output for Detailed Metrics:**

You can further parse the ping output to extract specific metrics like round-trip time (RTT) and packet loss. This can help in analyzing network performance over time.

```python
import subprocess
import re

def parse_ping_output(output):
    # Regular expression to extract the RTT
(round-trip time)
    rtt_pattern = r'time=(\d+\.\d+) ms'
    rtt_values = re.findall(rtt_pattern,
output)

    # Calculate the average RTT
    if rtt_values:
        rtt_values = list(map(float,
rtt_values))
```

```python
        avg_rtt   =   sum(rtt_values)   /
len(rtt_values)
        print(f"Average   RTT:   {avg_rtt}
ms")
    else:
        print("No RTT data found.")


    # Check for packet loss
    packet_loss_pattern = r'(\d+)% packet
loss'
    packet_loss                         =
re.findall(packet_loss_pattern, output)
    if packet_loss:
        print(f"Packet              loss:
{packet_loss[0]}%")


def ping_device(ip_address):
    result = subprocess.run(['ping', '-c',
'4', ip_address], stdout=subprocess.PIPE,
stderr=subprocess.PIPE)
    if result.returncode == 0:
        output                          =
result.stdout.decode('utf-8')
        parse_ping_output(output)
    else:
        print(f"Failed       to       ping
{ip_address}")


ping_device('192.168.1.1')
```

In this script:

- o **re.findall()** is used to extract round-trip times and packet loss from the ping output.
- o The script then calculates the average RTT and reports the packet loss percentage.

Collecting Metrics (e.g., Bandwidth, Latency, Packet Loss) with Python

Metrics such as bandwidth, latency, and packet loss are essential for monitoring network health and performance. Python can be used to automate the collection of these metrics and store the results for further analysis.

1. **Bandwidth Monitoring with SNMP:** As demonstrated earlier, you can use SNMP to collect bandwidth usage (bytes transmitted/received) from network interfaces. By continuously polling the device, you can monitor bandwidth over time and identify usage patterns.

```python
from pysnmp.hlapi import *
```

99

```
def get_bandwidth(ip_address, community):
    interface_oid_in                    =
'1.3.6.1.2.1.2.2.1.10'  # Incoming traffic
OID
    interface_oid_out                   =
'1.3.6.1.2.1.2.2.1.16'  # Outgoing traffic
OID

    iterator = getCmd(SnmpEngine(),

CommunityData(community),

UdpTransportTarget((ip_address, 161)),
                    ContextData(),

ObjectType(ObjectIdentity(interface_oid_i
n)),

ObjectType(ObjectIdentity(interface_oid_o
ut)))

    error_indication,         error_status,
error_index, var_binds = next(iterator)

    if error_indication:
        print(f"Error:
{error_indication}")
    elif error_status:
```

```
        print(f"Error           Status:
{error_status.prettyPrint()}")
    else:
        for var_bind in var_binds:
            print(f"Traffic         Data:
{var_bind}")

get_bandwidth('192.168.1.1', 'public')
```

2. **Network Health Dashboard:** You can build a simple network health dashboard that aggregates and visualizes the metrics you've collected (bandwidth, latency, packet loss). This can be done using Python's **matplotlib** or **plotly** libraries to create real-time graphs.

In this chapter, we've explored how Python can be used to automate the monitoring of network health by querying SNMP-enabled devices, pinging devices for latency and packet loss, and collecting essential performance metrics like bandwidth usage. With Python, you can create powerful tools for real-time network health checks, automate alerting, and gather actionable insights for optimizing your network's performance. In the next chapter, we will explore how to manage network failures and implement automatic remediation strategies.

CHAPTER 9

AUTOMATING TROUBLESHOOTING TASKS

Creating Python Scripts for Diagnosing Network Issues

Troubleshooting network issues can be a time-consuming task, especially when dealing with complex and large-scale networks. Automating troubleshooting tasks with Python can significantly reduce the time and effort required to diagnose and resolve network problems. This chapter will focus on creating Python scripts to help automate common network diagnostics such as pinging devices, tracerouting, checking interface statuses, and collecting logs for analysis.

Common Troubleshooting Tasks

1. **Pinging Devices:** One of the simplest and most effective tools for diagnosing network connectivity issues is **pinging**. Ping helps check whether a device is reachable across the network and measures

latency. Using Python, we can automate this process to ping multiple devices and log the results.

- o **Python Script for Pinging Multiple Devices:**

```python

import subprocess

def ping_device(ip_address):
    result = subprocess.run(['ping',
'-c',        '4',        ip_address],
stdout=subprocess.PIPE,
stderr=subprocess.PIPE)

    if result.returncode == 0:
        output               =
result.stdout.decode('utf-8')
        print(f"Ping to {ip_address}
successful!")
        print(output)
    else:
        print(f"Failed    to    ping
{ip_address}")

# List of devices to ping
devices       =       ['192.168.1.1',
'192.168.1.2', '192.168.1.3']
```

```
for device in devices:
    ping_device(device)
```

- o **Explanation**:
    - The script pings each device in the list of IP addresses.
    - It prints the output of the ping results, including any errors or packet loss information.

2. **Traceroute for Path Analysis: Traceroute** is another useful diagnostic tool that helps determine the path data takes from the source device to the destination. It's especially useful for identifying network hops that may be causing delays or packet loss.

   - o **Python Script for Tracerouting:**

```python
python

import subprocess

def traceroute_device(ip_address):
    result                =
subprocess.run(['traceroute',
ip_address], stdout=subprocess.PIPE,
stderr=subprocess.PIPE)
```

```
if result.returncode == 0:
    output =
result.stdout.decode('utf-8')
        print(f"Traceroute         to
{ip_address} successful!")
        print(output)
    else:
        print(f"Failed to traceroute
{ip_address}")


traceroute_device('8.8.8.8')       #
Example: Google Public DNS
```

- o **Explanation**:
  - The script runs the **traceroute** command to trace the route to a target device.
  - The output will show each hop along the path, which can be useful for diagnosing where packet loss or latency is occurring.

3. **Checking Network Interfaces:** Checking the status of interfaces on network devices can help diagnose issues related to connectivity, bandwidth, or errors on specific ports. Python scripts can be used to query SNMP-enabled devices for interface status and statistics.

   - o **Python Script for Checking Interface Status Using SNMP:**

```python
python

from pysnmp.hlapi import *

def
check_interface_status(ip_address,
community):
    interface_oid_status       =
'1.3.6.1.2.1.2.2.1.8'    # OID for
interface status (up/down)

    # Perform SNMP GET request
    iterator = getCmd(SnmpEngine(),

CommunityData(community),

UdpTransportTarget((ip_address,
161)),

ContextData(),

ObjectType(ObjectIdentity(interface
_oid_status)))

    error_indication, error_status,
error_index,      var_binds      =
next(iterator)

    if error_indication:
```

107

```
    print(f"Error:
{error_indication}")
        elif error_status:
        print(f"Error        Status:
{error_status.prettyPrint()}")
        else:
            for var_bind in var_binds:
                print(f"Interface
status: {var_bind}")


check_interface_status('192.168.1.1
', 'public')
```

o **Explanation**:

- The script queries an SNMP-enabled device (e.g., router or switch) for the status of its interfaces.

- **OID** 1.3.6.1.2.1.2.2.1.8 is used to fetch the operational status of network interfaces (e.g., up or down).

4. **Checking Device Logs:** Device logs are a crucial source of information when diagnosing network issues. In many cases, error messages, warnings, and status updates in the logs can point to the root cause of the problem. Automating the process of collecting and analyzing logs can save significant time.

o **Python Script for Collecting Logs via SSH:** You can use **Netmiko** to SSH into a device and collect logs automatically.

```python
python

from netmiko import ConnectHandler

def         collect_logs(ip_address,
community):
    device = {
        'device_type': 'cisco_ios',
        'host': ip_address,
        'username': 'admin',
        'password': 'password',
    }

    try:
        # Establish SSH connection
        net_connect             =
ConnectHandler(**device)

        # Collect logs    or  show
command output
        log_output              =
net_connect.send_command('show
logging')
        print(f"Logs           from
{ip_address}:")
```

109

```
print(log_output)

net_connect.disconnect()
```

```
except Exception as e:
    print(f"Failed    to    collect
logs from {ip_address}: {e}")
```

```
collect_logs('192.168.1.1',
'public')
```

- o **Explanation**:
  - The script connects to a Cisco router or switch via SSH and retrieves the logs using the `show logging` command.
  - You can replace `'show logging'` with any other device-specific command to collect different logs (e.g., system logs, interface logs).

Automating Logs Collection and Analysis

1. **Automated Log Collection from Multiple Devices:** To streamline the process of collecting logs from multiple devices, you can use a loop to SSH

into a list of devices, collect their logs, and store them in a local file or database.

```python

from netmiko import ConnectHandler

def collect_logs_from_devices(devices):
    for device in devices:
        try:
            net_connect = ConnectHandler(**device)
            log_output = net_connect.send_command('show logging')
            print(f"Logs from {device['host']}:\n{log_output}\n")
            with open(f"{device['host']}_logs.txt", "w") as file:
                file.write(log_output)
            net_connect.disconnect()

        except Exception as e:
            print(f"Failed to collect logs from {device['host']}: {e}")

devices = [
```

```
    {'device_type': 'cisco_ios', 'host':
'192.168.1.1',     'username':     'admin',
'password': 'password'},
    {'device_type': 'cisco_ios', 'host':
'192.168.1.2',     'username':     'admin',
'password': 'password'}
]


collect_logs_from_devices(devices)
```

- o **Explanation**:
  - ▪ The script loops through a list of devices, collects their logs, and saves them in individual log files.
  - ▪ This automation allows you to collect logs from multiple devices at once and store them for further analysis.

2. **Analyzing Collected Logs for Errors:** You can analyze the collected logs for specific error patterns or warnings. For instance, you could look for messages indicating interface failures, high CPU usage, or security events.

   - o **Python Script to Search Logs for Specific Errors:**

     ```
     python
     ```

```
def
search_logs_for_errors(log_file):
    with open(log_file, 'r') as
file:
        logs = file.readlines()

    for line in logs:
        if 'error' in line.lower()
or 'failed' in line.lower():
            print(f"Error    Found:
{line}")

# Example usage
search_logs_for_errors('192.168.1.1
_logs.txt')
```

- o **Explanation**:
  - The script reads a log file line by line and searches for the words "error" or "failed."
  - It prints the lines that contain error messages, allowing you to quickly identify potential issues.

3. **Automating Log Analysis with Regular Expressions:** If you need more advanced log analysis, Python's **re** (regular expressions) module can be used to search for specific patterns in the logs, such as interface errors, timeouts, or device reboots.

113

```python
python

import re

def analyze_logs_with_regex(log_file):
    with open(log_file, 'r') as file:
        logs = file.readlines()

    # Regular expression to match specific
error messages
    error_pattern = r'interface (\S+) .*
down'
    for line in logs:
        match = re.search(error_pattern,
line)
        if match:
            print(f"Interface
{match.group(1)} is down. Error: {line}")

# Example usage
analyze_logs_with_regex('192.168.1.1_logs
.txt')
```

- o **Explanation**:
    - This script uses a regular expression to find occurrences of interfaces that are down, which could indicate a connectivity issue.

114

In this chapter, we've explored how Python can be used to automate network troubleshooting tasks, such as pinging devices, performing traceroutes, checking interface statuses, and collecting logs for analysis. We've also shown how to automate the process of gathering logs from multiple devices and searching them for errors. By automating these tasks, you can significantly reduce the time spent on diagnosing network issues and quickly pinpoint the root cause of problems in your network. In the next chapter, we will explore network security automation and how to protect your network from vulnerabilities.

CHAPTER 10

MANAGING NETWORK SECURITY

Automating Firewall Rule Changes

Firewalls are a critical component in securing your network, protecting it from unauthorized access and malicious activities. Firewall rule management often involves adding, modifying, or deleting rules to control traffic between trusted and untrusted networks. Automating these tasks can save time and ensure consistency across multiple devices.

1. **Using Python to Automate Firewall Rule Changes:** Depending on the type of firewall you are working with (e.g., Cisco ASA, pfSense, or iptables), Python can be used to push configuration changes to the firewall. Below is an example of using **Netmiko** to automate firewall rule changes on a Cisco ASA firewall.

   o **Python Script to Add Firewall Rules (Cisco ASA Example):**

116

```python

from netmiko import ConnectHandler

def add_firewall_rule(ip_address,
username, password, rule_commands):
    device = {
        'device_type': 'cisco_asa',
        'host': ip_address,
        'username': username,
        'password': password,
    }

    try:
        # Connect to the firewall
device
        net_connect              =
ConnectHandler(**device)
        net_connect.enable()

        # Send the list of commands
to add the firewall rule
        output                   =
net_connect.send_config_set(rule_co
mmands)
        print(f"Firewall      rules
applied to {ip_address}:\n{output}")
```

```
        # Save the configuration to
the firewall
        net_connect.save_config()


        # Disconnect the session
        net_connect.disconnect()


    except Exception as e:
        print(f"Failed    to    add
firewall   rules   on   {ip_address}:
{e}")


# Example usage: Add a rule to allow
HTTP traffic
firewall_rules = [
    'access-list   outside_access_in
extended permit tcp any any eq 80',
    'access-group   outside_access_in
in interface outside'
]


add_firewall_rule('192.168.1.1',
'admin', 'password', firewall_rules)
```

- **Explanation**:
    - The script connects to a Cisco
      ASA firewall, sends a series of
      commands to add firewall rules
      (in this case, permitting HTTP

118

traffic), and saves the configuration.

- You can modify the list of commands (`firewall_rules`) to add other rules as needed.

2. **Automating Firewall Rule Changes for Multiple Devices:** When managing multiple firewalls across different sites, you can use Python to apply the same rule changes across all devices in a consistent manner.

```python
python

from netmiko import ConnectHandler

def
apply_firewall_rules_to_multiple_devices(
devices, rule_commands):
    for device in devices:
        try:
            # Connect to each device
            net_connect                =
ConnectHandler(**device)
            net_connect.enable()

            # Apply the configuration
```

119

```
        output                    =
net_connect.send_config_set(rule_commands
)
        print(f"Firewall rules applied
to {device['host']}:\n{output}")

        # Save the configuration
        net_connect.save_config()
        net_connect.disconnect()

    except Exception as e:
        print(f"Failed to apply rules
on {device['host']}: {e}")

devices = [
    {'device_type': 'cisco_asa', 'host':
'192.168.1.1',     'username':     'admin',
'password': 'password'},
    {'device_type': 'cisco_asa', 'host':
'192.168.1.2',     'username':     'admin',
'password': 'password'}
]

rules = [
    'access-list          outside_access_in
extended permit tcp any any eq 443',   #
HTTPS
    'access-group  outside_access_in   in
interface outside'
```

```
]

apply_firewall_rules_to_multiple_devices(
devices, rules)
```

- o **Explanation**:
  - ▪ This script automates the process of applying firewall rules to a list of devices, ensuring consistency and efficiency.

Python Scripts for Monitoring Network Security Events

Monitoring network security events is vital for detecting potential threats and malicious activities. Python can be used to automate the collection and analysis of security logs, track specific events, and alert administrators when suspicious activities are detected.

1. **Automating Security Event Log Collection:** Network devices like firewalls, routers, and intrusion detection systems (IDS) generate log files that record network activity and security events. Python can be used to collect and analyze these logs.
   - o **Python Script to Collect Logs from a Security Device (Firewall or IDS):**

121

```python
python

from netmiko import ConnectHandler

def collect_security_logs(device_ip,
username, password):
    device = {
        'device_type':  'cisco_asa',
# Adjust the device type if needed
        'host': device_ip,
        'username': username,
        'password': password,
    }

    try:
        # Establish connection
        net_connect                =
ConnectHandler(**device)
        net_connect.enable()

        #   Collect   security   logs
(example command for Cisco ASA)
        log_output                 =
net_connect.send_command('show
logging')
        print(f"Security   logs   from
{device_ip}:")
        print(log_output)
```

```
      #     Disconnect     after
collecting logs
      net_connect.disconnect()

   except Exception as e:
      print(f"Failed  to  collect
logs from {device_ip}: {e}")

collect_security_logs('192.168.1.1'
, 'admin', 'password')
```

- o **Explanation**:
  - The script connects to a Cisco ASA firewall and retrieves the logs using the `show logging` command.
  - You can adjust the command based on the specific security device you're working with (e.g., for IDS, you may query different commands or use APIs).

2. **Filtering and Analyzing Logs for Security Events:** Once you've collected logs, you can filter and analyze them for security events such as unauthorized access attempts, brute force attacks, or configuration changes.

  - o **Python Script to Search Logs for Suspicious Activity (e.g., Failed Login Attempts):**

123

```python

def
analyze_logs_for_security_events(lo
g_file):
    with  open(log_file,  'r')  as
file:
        logs = file.readlines()

    for line in logs:
        if 'authentication  failed'
in line.lower():  # Example security
event
            print(f"Security  Alert:
{line}")

# Example usage
analyze_logs_for_security_events('1
92.168.1.1_logs.txt')
```

- o **Explanation**:
  - ▪ The script reads through the log file and looks for specific phrases, such as "authentication failed," which could indicate a brute force attack or unauthorized access attempt.

- You can extend this analysis by looking for other patterns like "DENY" or "ACCESS REJECTED."

Integrating with Security Tools and Platforms (e.g., IDS/IPS, SIEM)

In addition to directly interacting with network devices, Python can be integrated with various security tools and platforms to automate network security management. This includes integrating with **IDS/IPS (Intrusion Detection/Prevention Systems)** for real-time monitoring, or **SIEM (Security Information and Event Management)** platforms for centralized log analysis.

1. **Integrating with IDS/IPS (e.g., Snort or Suricata):** IDS and IPS systems are used to monitor network traffic for signs of malicious activity. Snort and Suricata are two popular open-source IDS/IPS solutions. You can use Python to interface with these tools, collect alerts, and respond to events.

   o **Example Python Script to Collect Alerts from Snort:** If you're using Snort, you can collect its alerts by reading the alert file or querying its database via a network interface.

125

```python
python

def
collect_snort_alerts(snort_log_file
):
    with  open(snort_log_file,  'r')
as file:
        alerts = file.readlines()

    for alert in alerts:
        if 'alert' in alert.lower():
# Filter alerts for specific events
            print(f"Snort    Alert:
{alert}")

collect_snort_alerts('/var/log/snor
t/alert')
```

2. **Integrating with SIEM Platforms (e.g., Splunk or ELK):** SIEM platforms like **Splunk** and **ELK (Elasticsearch, Logstash, Kibana)** aggregate logs from various sources and provide advanced analysis and alerting features. You can use Python to interact with SIEM APIs to collect logs, search for security events, or automate reporting.

   o **Python Script to Query Splunk API for Security Events:**

126

```python
python

import requests

def query_splunk(splunk_url, token, query):
    headers = {
        'Authorization': f'Splunk {token}',
    }

    params = {
        'search': query,
        'output_mode': 'json'
    }

    response = requests.get(splunk_url, headers=headers, params=params)

    if response.status_code == 200:
        data = response.json()
        print(f"Splunk Search Results: {data}")
    else:
        print(f"Error querying Splunk: {response.status_code}")
```

```
splunk_url    =    'https://splunk-
server:8089/services/search/jobs/ex
port'
token = 'your-splunk-token-here'
query = 'search index=security_logs
"authentication failed"'

query_splunk(splunk_url,    token,
query)
```

- o **Explanation**:
  - This script queries the Splunk API for security events related to failed authentication attempts.
  - You can modify the query to search for different events based on your organization's security needs.

In this chapter, we've discussed how Python can be used to automate network security tasks, including firewall rule management, monitoring security events, and integrating with security tools such as IDS/IPS and SIEM platforms. Automating these tasks ensures quicker response times, better consistency, and more efficient security operations. In the next chapter, we will explore incident response automation and how to remediate network security incidents using Python.

CHAPTER 11

USING APIS FOR NETWORK AUTOMATION

Introduction to REST APIs in Networking

In the world of network automation, **APIs (Application Programming Interfaces)** are crucial for enabling devices to communicate with each other and with automation systems. **REST APIs (Representational State Transfer APIs)** have become the standard for interacting with networking devices and platforms due to their simplicity, scalability, and flexibility.

REST APIs are used to manage and automate network devices, retrieve data, and configure devices remotely. RESTful APIs rely on HTTP methods (GET, POST, PUT, DELETE) to perform operations on resources (devices, configurations, metrics). These APIs can be used to interact with a variety of network devices, including routers, switches, firewalls, and cloud-based services.

1. **Key Concepts of REST APIs:**
   - **Endpoints**: These are specific URLs that represent resources (e.g., a router's interface configuration, firewall rules).
   - **HTTP Methods**:
     - **GET**: Retrieve data (e.g., get the current configuration of a device).
     - **POST**: Create or modify data (e.g., add a new rule to a firewall).
     - **PUT**: Update existing data (e.g., modify an interface configuration).
     - **DELETE**: Remove data (e.g., delete an existing rule or configuration).
   - **Authentication**: REST APIs often require some form of authentication, such as API tokens, OAuth, or basic authentication, to ensure that only authorized users can access the device's resources.

2. **Benefits of Using REST APIs for Network Automation:**
   - **Ease of Integration**: Many modern network devices and platforms expose REST APIs,

130

making it easy to automate tasks across a range of devices.

- o **Scalability**: APIs allow for automation at scale, enabling the management of thousands of devices with minimal manual intervention.

- o **Flexibility**: APIs can be used to retrieve a variety of data types, from device status to configuration changes, and can be combined with other tools to enhance automation workflows.

Python Libraries for API Requests

Python provides several powerful libraries for interacting with REST APIs. These libraries allow you to send HTTP requests, handle responses, and process the data returned from the API. Below are the two most commonly used libraries for making API requests in Python:

1. **Requests Library:** The **Requests** library is the most popular Python library for making HTTP requests. It simplifies the process of interacting with REST APIs and handling responses.

   - o **Installation:**

   ```bash
   bash
   ```

131

```
pip install requests
```

o **Basic Example of Using Requests to Interact with an API:**

```python
python

import requests

# Define the API endpoint
api_url                          =
'https://api.example.com/v1/devices
'

# Send GET request to retrieve data
response = requests.get(api_url)

# Check if the request was successful
if response.status_code == 200:
    data = response.json()   # Parse
the JSON response
    print("API Response:", data)
else:
    print(f"Error:
{response.status_code}")
```

o **Explanation**:

- **requests.get()** sends a GET request to the API endpoint.
- **response.json()** converts the JSON response into a Python dictionary for easier processing.
- The **status_code** checks if the request was successful (HTTP status code 200).

2. **Urllib Library: Urllib** is another built-in Python library used for working with URLs and sending HTTP requests. It provides more granular control over HTTP connections but is slightly more complex than the Requests library.

   o **Basic Example of Using Urllib to Interact with an API:**

```python
python

import urllib.request
import json

# Define the API endpoint
api_url                               =
'https://api.example.com/v1/devices
'

# Send GET request
```

```
with urllib.request.urlopen(api_url)
as response:
    data                        =
json.loads(response.read())  # Parse
the JSON response
    print("API Response:", data)
```

- o **Explanation**:
  - **urllib.request.urlopen()** sends the GET request.
  - **json.loads()** parses the JSON response into a Python dictionary.

While **Requests** is more user-friendly, **Urllib** offers more flexibility and is part of the Python standard library, making it a good choice for certain use cases.

Automating Interactions with Network Devices through APIs

Now that we have learned how to send HTTP requests and process responses, let's dive into how we can use APIs to automate interactions with network devices. Many modern network devices expose REST APIs to enable remote management, configuration, and monitoring.

134

1. **Example: Interacting with a Cisco REST API to Get Device Information**

Cisco devices running **IOS XE** or **NX-OS** can be managed through their REST APIs. Here's an example of how you can use Python to retrieve information from a Cisco device via its REST API:

```python
python

import requests
from requests.auth import HTTPBasicAuth

# Cisco device REST API endpoint
api_url                    =
'https://192.168.1.1/api/v1/device'

# Authentication credentials
username = 'admin'
password = 'password'

#  Send  GET  request  with  basic
authentication
response    =    requests.get(api_url,
auth=HTTPBasicAuth(username,    password),
verify=False)

if response.status_code == 200:
```

```
    device_info = response.json()  # Parse
JSON response
    print("Device            Information:",
device_info)
else:
    print(f"Failed   to   retrieve   device
information: {response.status_code}")
```

- o **Explanation**:
  - **HTTPBasicAuth(username, password)** handles basic authentication for the API.
  - The **verify=False** argument is used to disable SSL certificate verification (useful in testing environments).
  - The script retrieves device information from a Cisco device, such as model and serial number.

2. **Example: Automating Configuration Changes on a Network Device via API**

Some network devices allow you to automate configuration changes via their REST APIs. Here's an example of how to use an API to change the hostname of a device:

```
python
```

```python
import requests
from requests.auth import HTTPBasicAuth

# Device API endpoint
api_url                          =
'https://192.168.1.1/api/v1/system/hostna
me'

# New hostname for the device
new_hostname = 'NewRouterName'

# Authentication credentials
username = 'admin'
password = 'password'

# Data payload for updating the hostname
data = {
    'hostname': new_hostname
}

# Send PUT request to update the hostname
response       =       requests.put(api_url,
json=data,     auth=HTTPBasicAuth(username,
password), verify=False)

if response.status_code == 200:
    print(f"Hostname        updated        to
{new_hostname}")
```

```
else:
    print(f"Failed   to   update   hostname:
{response.status_code}")
```

- o **Explanation**:
  - **requests.put()** sends a PUT request to the device's API to update its hostname.
  - The data is sent in JSON format, which is a common format for APIs.
  - The script checks the response status code to ensure the update was successful.

3. **Example: Retrieving Interface Status from a Network Device via API**

Many network devices expose interface data via their REST APIs. Here's an example script to retrieve the status of all interfaces on a device:

```python
import requests
from requests.auth import HTTPBasicAuth

# Device API endpoint
api_url                                    =
'https://192.168.1.1/api/v1/interfaces'
```

```
# Authentication credentials
username = 'admin'
password = 'password'

# Send GET request to retrieve interface
data
response       =       requests.get(api_url,
auth=HTTPBasicAuth(username,     password),
verify=False)

if response.status_code == 200:
    interfaces = response.json()   # Parse
JSON response
    for interface in interfaces['items']:
        print(f"Interface
{interface['name']}                      is
{interface['status']}")
else:
    print(f"Failed  to  retrieve  interface
data: {response.status_code}")
```

- o **Explanation**:
  - ▪ The script queries the device for its interface status and prints the status of each interface.
  - ▪ The API response is assumed to return a JSON object containing a list of interfaces under the items key.

139

Best Practices for Using APIs in Network Automation

1. Use Secure Authentication Methods:

- o Always use secure authentication methods (e.g., OAuth, API tokens) rather than passing plain-text credentials in your scripts.
- o Many APIs offer token-based authentication for better security.

2. Error Handling:

- o Ensure proper error handling is in place to deal with failed requests, timeouts, and other API errors.
- o Always check the **HTTP status codes** (e.g., 200 for success, 400 for bad request, 404 for not found) to handle errors appropriately.

3. Rate Limiting:

- o Be aware of API rate limits, which restrict the number of requests you can make in a given period.
- o Consider implementing **retry logic** and **backoff strategies** if the API enforces rate limits.

4. API Documentation:

- o Always refer to the API documentation provided by the device manufacturer. This will help you understand available endpoints, authentication methods, and usage limits.

5. **Logging and Auditing:**

o Implement logging for all interactions with APIs to ensure traceability. This will help you debug issues and maintain an audit trail of configuration changes or data retrieval.

In this chapter, we've introduced **REST APIs** in networking and demonstrated how Python can be used to automate interactions with network devices through APIs. By using Python libraries like **Requests** and **Urllib**, you can automate configuration changes, retrieve device information, and interact with network devices efficiently. These capabilities make Python an essential tool for modern network automation workflows. In the next chapter, we will explore how to integrate network automation tasks with cloud platforms for even more scalability and flexibility.

CHAPTER 12

DATA COLLECTION AND ANALYSIS

Automating Data Collection from Network Devices

In network automation, one of the key tasks is to collect relevant data from network devices (routers, switches, firewalls, etc.) to monitor their health, performance, and security. Automating the process of data collection ensures that important metrics, such as interface status, traffic statistics, and device health, are collected regularly and consistently.

1. **Automating Data Collection via SNMP: SNMP (Simple Network Management Protocol)** is widely used for collecting performance data from network devices. Python's **PySNMP** library allows you to automate SNMP requests and retrieve valuable data from devices.

   Here's a basic example of how to automate data collection for network interface statistics:

```python
python

from pysnmp.hlapi import *

def   collect_data_from_device(ip_address,
community):
    interface_oid_in                      =
'1.3.6.1.2.1.2.2.1.10'  # OID for incoming
traffic (bytes)
    interface_oid_out                     =
'1.3.6.1.2.1.2.2.1.16'  # OID for outgoing
traffic (bytes)

    iterator = getCmd(SnmpEngine(),

CommunityData(community),

UdpTransportTarget((ip_address, 161)),
                    ContextData(),

ObjectType(ObjectIdentity(interface_oid_i
n)),

ObjectType(ObjectIdentity(interface_oid_o
ut)))

    error_indication,         error_status,
error_index, var_binds = next(iterator)
```

143

```
if error_indication:
    print(f"Error:
{error_indication}")
    elif error_status:
        print(f"Error          Status:
{error_status.prettyPrint()}")
    else:
        for var_bind in var_binds:
            print(f"Traffic          Data:
{var_bind}")

# Example usage:
collect_data_from_device('192.168.1.1',
'public')
```

- o **Explanation**:
  - The script queries the network device for incoming and outgoing traffic statistics using the **OID** (Object Identifier) associated with traffic counters.
  - It then processes the returned data and prints it to the console.

2. **Automating Data Collection via REST APIs:** Many modern network devices expose REST APIs that allow you to collect data more efficiently. Here's an example of how you can automate data collection from a network device using its REST API:

```python
python

import requests
from requests.auth import HTTPBasicAuth

def collect_data_from_api(ip_address,
username, password):
    api_url                          =
f'https://{ip_address}/api/v1/interfaces'
    response    =    requests.get(api_url,
auth=HTTPBasicAuth(username,    password),
verify=False)

    if response.status_code == 200:
        data = response.json()
        for interface in data['items']:
            print(f"Interface
{interface['name']}                        is
{interface['status']}")
    else:
        print(f"Failed   to   collect   data
from                       {ip_address}:
{response.status_code}")

# Example usage:
collect_data_from_api('192.168.1.1',
'admin', 'password')
```

o **Explanation**:

145

- This script uses the **requests** library to interact with the REST API of the network device, collecting interface data like status and name.
- The data is retrieved in JSON format, and the script processes and prints relevant information.

Parsing and Analyzing Collected Data with Python

Once data is collected from network devices, it's important to parse and analyze it to extract meaningful insights. Python offers several powerful libraries for parsing data (e.g., **JSON, XML**) and performing analysis, such as identifying trends, detecting anomalies, or calculating performance metrics.

1. **Parsing JSON Data:** When interacting with REST APIs, the data is often returned in **JSON** format. Python's built-in `json` library can be used to parse this data into Python dictionaries for easy manipulation.

```python
```

```
import json

def parse_json_data(json_data):
    # Parse the JSON string into a Python
dictionary
    data = json.loads(json_data)

    # Example: print the name and status of
each interface
    for interface in data['interfaces']:
        print(f"Interface:
{interface['name']},                Status:
{interface['status']}")

# Example JSON data (typically fetched from
a REST API)
json_data    =    '{"interfaces":    [{"name":
"eth0", "status": "up"}, {"name": "eth1",
"status": "down"}]}'
parse_json_data(json_data)
```

- o **Explanation**:
  - ▪ The script parses the provided **JSON** data using `json.loads()` and then iterates over the interfaces to print their status.

2. **Analyzing Performance Metrics:** Once data is collected and parsed, you can analyze it to identify

147

network performance metrics such as bandwidth usage, packet loss, latency, and error rates.

Here's an example of how you might calculate the **average bandwidth usage** for network interfaces:

```python
def
analyze_bandwidth_usage(incoming_traffic,
outgoing_traffic):
    total_traffic = incoming_traffic +
outgoing_traffic
    average_traffic = total_traffic / 2
    print(f"Average bandwidth usage:
{average_traffic} bytes")

# Example data: incoming and outgoing
traffic in bytes
incoming_traffic = 5000000  # 5MB
outgoing_traffic = 3000000  # 3MB
analyze_bandwidth_usage(incoming_traffic,
outgoing_traffic)
```

- o **Explanation**:
  - The function calculates the total and average traffic by summing the incoming and outgoing traffic and dividing by two.

148

3. **Analyzing Latency and Packet Loss:** Python can also be used to analyze network performance data, such as latency and packet loss, which are common indicators of network health.

Here's how you might process **ping results** (from a previous chapter) to calculate average latency and detect packet loss:

python

```
import re

def analyze_ping_output(ping_output):
    # Regex to find latency (time=xx.xx ms)
    latencies                          =
re.findall(r'time=(\d+\.\d+)          ms',
ping_output)

    if latencies:
        avg_latency    =    sum(map(float,
latencies)) / len(latencies)
        print(f"Average          Latency:
{avg_latency} ms")
    else:
        print("No latency data found.")
```

```
    # Check for packet loss (e.g., 10%
packet loss)
    packet_loss    =    re.search(r'(\d+)%
packet loss', ping_output)
    if packet_loss:
        print(f"Packet              Loss:
{packet_loss.group(1)}%")
    else:
        print("No packet loss detected.")


# Example ping output (usually comes from
a system's ping command)
ping_output = """
PING   192.168.1.1   (192.168.1.1)   56(84)
bytes of data.
64  bytes  from  192.168.1.1:  icmp_seq=1
ttl=64 time=2.19 ms
64  bytes  from  192.168.1.1:  icmp_seq=2
ttl=64 time=2.15 ms
64  bytes  from  192.168.1.1:  icmp_seq=3
ttl=64 time=2.13 ms
64  bytes  from  192.168.1.1:  icmp_seq=4
ttl=64 time=2.18 ms

--- 192.168.1.1 ping statistics ---
4  packets  transmitted,  4  received,  0%
packet loss, time 3003ms
rtt            min/avg/max/mdev            =
2.134/2.169/2.199/0.025 ms
```

```
"""
analyze_ping_output(ping_output)
```

- o **Explanation**:
    - ▪ The script uses regular expressions to extract latency values and packet loss percentage from the output of a **ping** command.
    - ▪ It calculates the average latency and prints the packet loss percentage.

Generating Reports from Collected Data

After collecting and analyzing network data, it's often necessary to generate reports that summarize the findings in a readable format. Python can automate the generation of reports in various formats, including **text files**, **CSV**, and **PDF**.

1. **Generating CSV Reports:** CSV files are widely used for reporting because they are easy to read and manipulate in spreadsheet software. Python's **csv** module makes it easy to create CSV reports from network data.

```
python
```

```
import csv

def generate_csv_report(data, filename):
    with open(filename, mode='w',
newline='') as file:
        writer = csv.writer(file)
        writer.writerow(['Device',
'Interface', 'Status', 'Traffic'])
        for row in data:
            writer.writerow(row)

# Example data (Device, Interface, Status,
Traffic)
network_data = [
    ['Router1', 'GigabitEthernet0/1',
'up', '500MB'],
    ['Router2', 'GigabitEthernet0/2',
'down', '0MB'],
]

generate_csv_report(network_data,
'network_report.csv')
```

- o **Explanation**:
  - The script generates a **CSV** report containing device names, interface statuses, and traffic data. The data is

written   to   a   file   called
`network_report.csv`.

2. **Generating PDF Reports:** Python libraries like **ReportLab** can be used to generate PDF reports, which are useful for sharing formal reports with stakeholders.

- o **Installation:**

```bash
bash
```

```bash
pip install reportlab
```

- o **Basic Example of Generating a PDF Report:**

```python
python
```

```python
from reportlab.lib.pagesizes import letter
from reportlab.pdfgen import canvas

def      generate_pdf_report(data,
filename):
    c    =    canvas.Canvas(filename,
pagesize=letter)
    c.drawString(100,  750,  "Network
Performance Report")
```

```
y_position = 730
for row in data:
    c.drawString(100,
y_position, f"{row[0]} - {row[1]} -
{row[2]} - {row[3]}")
    y_position -= 20

    c.save()

# Example data
network_data = [
    ['Router1',
'GigabitEthernet0/1',              'up',
'500MB'],
    ['Router2',
'GigabitEthernet0/2',              'down',
'0MB'],
]

generate_pdf_report(network_data,
'network_report.pdf')
```

o **Explanation**:

- The script uses **ReportLab** to generate a simple **PDF** report with network performance data.

154

In this chapter, we have explored how to automate data collection from network devices, parse and analyze the data using Python, and generate reports from the collected data. These tasks are fundamental to network automation, helping network administrators monitor performance, identify issues, and share important metrics with stakeholders. In the next chapter, we will explore how to integrate network automation with cloud platforms to scale network operations effectively.

CHAPTER 13

AUTOMATING NETWORK CONFIGURATION BACKUPS

Importance of Backup Configurations

Network configurations are essential to the operation of any network device. These configurations define how devices behave, interact with each other, and manage network traffic. Whether you are working with routers, switches, firewalls, or any other network hardware, having reliable backups of these configurations is critical for several reasons:

1. **Disaster Recovery:**
   o Network devices can fail due to hardware malfunctions, software bugs, or misconfigurations. A backup allows you to quickly restore the device to a working state, minimizing downtime.
2. **Configuration Rollback:**
   o If a new configuration change causes issues or breaks the network, having a backup allows you

to revert to the previous, stable configuration without manually re-entering settings.

3. **Consistency Across Devices:**

   o In large networks, multiple devices need to have similar configurations. Automated backups ensure that configurations are consistent and can be restored on similar devices if needed.

4. **Compliance and Auditing:**

   o Many organizations are required to maintain copies of network configurations for compliance purposes. Regular backups help maintain an accurate record of network configurations for auditing and regulatory requirements.

Automating the backup process ensures that you always have up-to-date backups stored safely and eliminates the need for manual intervention.

Python Scripts to Back Up Network Device Configurations

Python can be used to automate the backup of network device configurations, whether you are interacting with the devices over SSH (using **Netmiko**) or via REST APIs. Below are examples of using Python to back up configurations from different types of network devices.

1. **Backing Up Cisco Device Configurations (using Netmiko)**

Cisco devices, such as routers and switches, typically run **IOS** (Internetwork Operating System), which supports configuration backups through CLI commands. The **Netmiko** library allows Python to interact with Cisco devices over SSH and automate this process.

- **Example: Backup Cisco Router Configuration Using SSH (Netmiko)**:

```python
from netmiko import ConnectHandler
import time

def backup_cisco_config(ip_address, username, password, backup_dir):
    device = {
        'device_type': 'cisco_ios',
        'host': ip_address,
        'username': username,
        'password': password,
        'secret': password,       # Enable password, if required
    }
```

158

```
try:
    # Connect to the Cisco device
    net_connect         =
ConnectHandler(**device)
    net_connect.enable()

    # Send command to back up the
configuration
    config              =
net_connect.send_command('show
running-config')

    # Save the configuration to
a file
    timestamp           =
time.strftime("%Y%m%d-%H%M%S")
    backup_filename     =
f"{backup_dir}/config_backup_{ip_ad
dress}_{timestamp}.txt"

    with    open(backup_filename,
'w') as file:
        file.write(config)

    print(f"Configuration backup
saved to {backup_filename}")

    # Disconnect after backup
```

```
net_connect.disconnect()

    except Exception as e:
        print(f"Failed to back up
configuration from {ip_address}:
{e}")

# Example usage
backup_cisco_config('192.168.1.1',
'admin',                'password',
'/path/to/backups')
```

- o **Explanation**:
  - The script connects to a Cisco device using **Netmiko** and retrieves the running configuration using the `show running-config` command.
  - The configuration is saved to a text file, with the filename including the device IP address and timestamp for easy identification.
  - The backup is stored in a specified directory (`/path/to/backups`), and the device session is closed afterward.

2. **Backing Up Juniper Device Configurations (using PyEZ)**

For **Juniper** devices (running **Junos OS**), **PyEZ** is a Python library that can be used to interact with the device's REST APIs or over SSH to back up configurations.

- ○ **Installation:**

```bash
pip install junos-eznc
```

- ○ **Example: Backup Juniper Router Configuration Using PyEZ:**

```python
from jnpr.junos import Device
from jnpr.junos.exception import ConnectError

def backup_juniper_config(ip_address, username, password, backup_dir):
    try:
        # Connect to the Juniper device
        dev = Device(host=ip_address, user=username, passwd=password)
```

161

```
        dev.open()

        # Get the configuration
        config                =
dev.rpc.get_config()

        # Save the configuration to
a file
        timestamp             =
time.strftime("%Y%m%d-%H%M%S")
        backup_filename       =
f"{backup_dir}/config_backup_{ip_ad
dress}_{timestamp}.xml"

        with   open(backup_filename,
'w') as file:
            file.write(str(config))

        print(f"Configuration backup
saved to {backup_filename}")

        # Close the connection
        dev.close()

    except ConnectError as e:
        print(f"Failed to connect to
{ip_address}: {e}")
    except Exception as e:
```

```
        print(f"Error  during  backup
from {ip_address}: {e}")


# Example usage
backup_juniper_config('192.168.1.1'
,        'admin',        'password',
'/path/to/backups')
```

o **Explanation**:

- The script connects to a **Juniper** device using **PyEZ**, retrieves the configuration using the `get_config()` method, and saves it as an XML file.
- The backup file includes the device's IP address and timestamp, and the file is stored in the specified backup directory.

Automating Backup Scheduling and Storage

Once you have a script for backing up network device configurations, you can automate the scheduling of these backups to run at regular intervals. You can use **cron jobs** (on Linux/Mac) or **Task Scheduler** (on Windows) to schedule the backup scripts. Additionally, you can store backups securely and organize them efficiently.

163

1. **Scheduling Backups with Cron (Linux/Mac)**

You can set up a cron job to run the backup script at regular intervals, such as daily or weekly. To schedule a cron job:

-   Open the cron job editor by running:

```bash
crontab -e
```

-   Add a cron job to run the backup script every day at midnight:

```bash
0  0  *  *  *  /usr/bin/python3 /path/to/your_backup_script.py
```

-   **Explanation**:
    -   The cron job is configured to execute the Python script every day at midnight. You can adjust the schedule based on your needs (e.g., weekly, monthly).

2. **Scheduling Backups with Task Scheduler (Windows)**

On Windows, you can use **Task Scheduler** to automate the execution of backup scripts. Here's how to set it up:

- o Open **Task Scheduler** and create a new task.
- o Set the task trigger to run at a specific time (e.g., daily at midnight).
- o In the "Actions" section, select "Start a Program" and specify the path to the Python executable and your backup script (e.g., `python.exe C:\path\to\your_backup_script.py`).

3. **Storing Backups Securely**

Storing backups securely is vital to prevent data loss or unauthorized access. Some best practices include:

- o **Encryption**: Encrypt backups to ensure their confidentiality. You can use tools like **GPG** or **OpenSSL** to encrypt the backup files before storing them.
- o **Off-site Storage**: Consider using cloud storage (e.g., **AWS S3**, **Google Cloud Storage**, or **Dropbox**) to store backups off-site, ensuring redundancy in case of local failures.

165

o **Version Control**: Store multiple versions of configuration backups to allow you to roll back to previous configurations. You can implement version control by appending timestamps or version numbers to backup filenames.

o **Example: Storing Backups in AWS S3 Using Boto3**:

python

```
import boto3
from    botocore.exceptions    import
NoCredentialsError

def upload_backup_to_s3(backup_file,
bucket_name):
    s3 = boto3.client('s3')
    try:
        s3.upload_file(backup_file,
bucket_name,
backup_file.split('/')[-1])
        print(f"Backup uploaded to
S3 bucket {bucket_name}")
    except NoCredentialsError:
        print("Credentials      not
available for S3 upload")
    except Exception as e:
```

166

```
        print(f"Error  uploading  to
S3: {e}")


# Example usage
upload_backup_to_s3('/path/to/backu
p/config_backup_192.168.1.1_2023032
2.txt', 'my-s3-bucket')
```

o **Explanation**:

- The script uses **Boto3**, the AWS SDK for Python, to upload backup files to an **S3 bucket**. This ensures your backups are stored securely in the cloud.

In this chapter, we've learned how to automate network configuration backups using Python, making it easier to manage and secure network devices. By utilizing tools like **Netmiko** and **PyEZ**, we can retrieve device configurations and save them automatically. Additionally, we discussed how to schedule backups with cron or Task Scheduler, and securely store backups in cloud storage platforms like **AWS S3**. Automating configuration backups ensures that your network configurations are always recoverable, even in the event of device failure or misconfiguration.

CHAPTER 14

SCHEDULED TASKS AND AUTOMATION

Using Python for Scheduled Tasks in Network Automation

In network automation, many tasks need to be executed at regular intervals, such as performing routine configuration checks, monitoring network performance, collecting data, and applying updates. Python provides a simple and efficient way to automate these tasks using scheduling tools like **cron jobs** on Linux/macOS or **Task Scheduler** on Windows.

By automating these tasks, network administrators can ensure that critical processes run without human intervention, reduce the risk of manual errors, and maintain a consistent and efficient network management workflow.

Automating Periodic Configuration Checks and Updates

1. **Automating Configuration Backups:** One of the most common network automation tasks is ensuring

168

regular backups of device configurations. We can use Python to back up configurations on a scheduled basis. Here's a simple example of how to automate a **Cisco device configuration backup**:

```python
python

from netmiko import ConnectHandler
import time

def         backup_cisco_config(ip_address,
username, password, backup_dir):
    device = {
        'device_type': 'cisco_ios',
        'host': ip_address,
        'username': username,
        'password': password,
        'secret': password,    # Enable
password, if required
    }

    try:
        # Connect to the Cisco device
        net_connect                      =
ConnectHandler(**device)
        net_connect.enable()

        # Send command to back up the
configuration
```

```
        config                        =
net_connect.send_command('show    running-
config')

        # Save the configuration to a file
        timestamp = time.strftime("%Y%m%d-
%H%M%S")
        backup_filename               =
f"{backup_dir}/config_backup_{ip_address}
_{timestamp}.txt"

        with open(backup_filename, 'w') as
file:
            file.write(config)

        print(f"Configuration backup saved
to {backup_filename}")

        # Disconnect after backup
        net_connect.disconnect()

    except Exception as e:
        print(f"Failed    to    back    up
configuration from {ip_address}: {e}")

# Example usage
backup_cisco_config('192.168.1.1',
'admin', 'password', '/path/to/backups')
```

o **Explanation**:

170

- The script connects to a Cisco device, retrieves the **running configuration**, and saves it to a file with a timestamp.
- The backup file is stored in a specified directory for easy management.

2. **Automating Periodic Network Performance Checks:** For continuous network health monitoring, you can automate periodic checks for latency, bandwidth usage, and packet loss. Here's a basic example using **ping** to check the latency of a device:

```python
import subprocess
import time

def ping_device(ip_address):
    # Execute the ping command
    result = subprocess.run(['ping', '-c',
'4', ip_address], stdout=subprocess.PIPE,
stderr=subprocess.PIPE)

    if result.returncode == 0:
        output                       =
result.stdout.decode('utf-8')
        print(f"Ping    to    {ip_address}
successful!")
        print(output)
```

171

```
else:
        print(f"Failed        to        ping
{ip_address}")


def schedule_ping():
    while True:
        print("Pinging    192.168.1.1    to
check network health...")
        ping_device('192.168.1.1')
        time.sleep(3600)  # Wait for 1 hour
before running the next ping check


schedule_ping()
```

- o **Explanation**:
  - The script runs a **ping** command to check the connectivity and latency to a network device (192.168.1.1).
  - It automatically repeats the process every hour using **time.sleep(3600)**, ensuring continuous monitoring.

3. **Automating Configuration Updates:** You can use Python to check for configuration drift and automatically apply updates based on changes. For example, you could periodically check the running configuration of a network device and compare it against a stored baseline configuration. If changes

172

are detected, the script can apply the necessary updates or restore the configuration.

```python
def
check_and_update_configuration(ip_address
, current_config, username, password):
    device = {
        'device_type': 'cisco_ios',
        'host': ip_address,
        'username': username,
        'password': password,
        'secret': password,
    }

    try:
        # Connect to the device
        net_connect                      =
ConnectHandler(**device)
        net_connect.enable()

        # Get the current configuration
        device_config                    =
net_connect.send_command('show    running-
config')
```

173

```
        # Compare with the baseline
configuration (simplified for this
example)
        if device_config !=
current_config:
            print(f"Configuration drift
detected on {ip_address}. Updating...")

net_connect.send_config_set(current_confi
g.splitlines())  # Apply updates
            print(f"Configuration updated
on {ip_address}")
        else:
            print(f"No changes needed for
{ip_address}")

        net_connect.disconnect()

    except Exception as e:
        print(f"Error during configuration
update on {ip_address}: {e}")

# Example usage
current_config = '''hostname Router1
interface GigabitEthernet0/1
ip address 192.168.2.1 255.255.255.0
no shutdown'''
check_and_update_configuration('192.168.1
.1', current_config, 'admin', 'password')
```

174

- o **Explanation**:
  - The script compares the running configuration of the device with the baseline configuration (`current_config`).
  - If differences are detected, it applies the necessary updates to the device.

Task Automation Using Cron Jobs or Windows Task Scheduler

Once you have Python scripts ready to automate tasks such as configuration backups or network performance checks, you can schedule these tasks to run automatically at specific intervals using either **cron jobs** (on Linux/macOS) or **Windows Task Scheduler**.

1. **Scheduling Tasks with Cron Jobs (Linux/macOS)**

   Cron is a powerful tool in Unix-like operating systems that allows you to schedule tasks to run at specific times or intervals. You can use **cron** to schedule your Python scripts.

   - o Open the **crontab** editor:

```bash
bash
```

175

```
crontab -e
```

- o Add a cron job to run your backup script daily at midnight:

```
bash
```

```
0  0  *  *  *  /usr/bin/python3
/path/to/backup_script.py
```

- o **Explanation**:
  - The cron job will run the backup script every day at midnight (00:00). You can customize the schedule (e.g., hourly, weekly) based on your needs.
- o To view all scheduled cron jobs, use:

```
bash
```

```
crontab -l
```

2. Scheduling Tasks with Windows Task Scheduler

Task Scheduler is a tool in Windows that allows you to schedule scripts or programs to run at specified times. You can set it up to run Python scripts at regular intervals.

- o Open **Task Scheduler** and click on **Create Basic Task**.

- o Give the task a name (e.g., "Network Backup Task").

- o Choose the trigger (e.g., Daily, Weekly) and set the time for the task to run.

- o In the **Action** step, select **Start a Program** and browse to the Python executable (e.g., `python.exe`), and add the path to your Python script as the argument (e.g., `C:\path\to\backup_script.py`).

- o **Explanation**:

  - This allows you to schedule tasks (like configuration backups or network checks) to run at specified times without needing to manually trigger them.

Best Practices for Task Automation

1. **Logging:**

   - o Ensure that each scheduled task logs its activities (successes, failures, and errors). This allows you to track what happened during each automated task and troubleshoot any issues that arise.

Example:

```
python
```

```
import logging
logging.basicConfig(filename='/path/to/lo
gfile.log', level=logging.INFO)
logging.info("Task started")
```

2. Email Notifications:

- o Consider adding email notifications to alert you when a task completes or encounters an issue. You can use libraries like **smtplib** to send email alerts when tasks fail or succeed.

3. Error Handling:

- o Ensure proper error handling in your Python scripts so that any issues (e.g., network connectivity, permission errors) are caught, logged, and communicated (via email or logs).

4. Security:

- o Always secure credentials (e.g., usernames, passwords) when using them in automation scripts. Consider using environment variables, encrypted configuration files, or password managers to keep sensitive data safe.

5. Testing:

o   Test your scripts thoroughly before scheduling
them. Run them manually first to ensure that they
work as expected and produce the desired
outcomes.

In this chapter, we've learned how to automate network tasks using Python, including configuration backups, periodic checks, and configuration updates. Additionally, we covered how to schedule these tasks to run automatically using cron jobs or Task Scheduler. Automating network management tasks not only saves time but also ensures consistency and reliability in your network operations. In the next chapter, we will explore how to integrate network automation with cloud platforms for more scalable and flexible operations.

4o mini

CHAPTER 15

WORKING WITH NETWORK CONFIGURATION MANAGEMENT TOOLS

Overview of Configuration Management Tools

Configuration management tools are essential in modern network automation, allowing network administrators to define, deploy, and manage configurations across devices in a repeatable, reliable, and efficient manner. These tools provide a framework for automating device configuration, ensuring consistency, and facilitating easier management at scale.

Two of the most widely used configuration management tools in network automation are **Ansible** and **SaltStack**. These tools are designed to simplify the process of managing configurations across multiple network devices, reducing the complexity of manual configuration updates.

1. **Ansible:**

- o **Overview**: **Ansible** is an open-source automation tool that uses a simple, agentless, and declarative approach to manage configurations. It uses **Playbooks** (written in YAML) to define tasks and configurations that should be applied to target devices. Ansible is widely popular in the IT and networking space for its ease of use and scalability.
- o **Key Features**:
  - **Agentless**: Ansible does not require any special agents to be installed on target devices; it communicates via SSH or APIs.
  - **Idempotence**: Ansible ensures that tasks are executed only when necessary (i.e., if the configuration is already in the desired state, Ansible will not reapply it).
  - **Extensive Support**: Ansible supports a wide range of network devices, including Cisco, Juniper, Arista, and more.

2. **SaltStack:**
  - o **Overview**: **SaltStack**, or simply **Salt**, is another popular automation tool designed for configuration management, orchestration, and remote execution. Salt is known for its high-

performance capabilities, scalability, and real-time remote execution.

- o **Key Features**:
  - **High-speed communication**: Salt uses a central master-slave architecture to manage multiple devices in real time.
  - **Flexibility**: Salt provides both push and pull models for configuration management.
  - **Python Integration**: SaltStack can be integrated with Python to extend functionality, especially for network automation tasks.

Both Ansible and SaltStack provide native support for network automation, making them ideal for managing large, diverse networks with minimal human intervention.

Integrating Python Scripts with These Tools for Automation

While both Ansible and SaltStack provide their own command-line tools and APIs, integrating **Python** with these tools can provide additional flexibility, allowing you to leverage Python's powerful libraries and automation capabilities within the broader workflow.

1. **Integrating Python with Ansible**:

Ansible provides an API called **Ansible Python API**, which allows you to programmatically control and interact with Ansible from Python scripts. This is useful when you need to trigger Ansible tasks from within a Python script or integrate with other systems.

- o **Installation**: You can install the `ansible` library and `ansible-runner` (a Python library for running Ansible playbooks) using **pip**:

  ```bash
  pip install ansible ansible-runner
  ```

- o **Example: Running an Ansible Playbook from a Python Script**:

  ```python
  import ansible.runner
  ```

183

```python
def
run_ansible_playbook(playbook_path,
inventory_file):
    # Define the options for the
Ansible runner
    options = {
        'playbook': playbook_path,
        'inventory': inventory_file
    }

    # Execute the playbook
    runner                        =
ansible.runner.Runner(options)
    results = runner.run()

    # Print the results
    if results['status'] == 'ok':
        print("Playbook    executed
successfully.")
    else:
        print(f"Playbook  execution
failed         with         error:
{results['status']}")

# Example usage
run_ansible_playbook('/path/to/play
book.yml', '/path/to/inventory')
```

○ **Explanation**:

184

- This script demonstrates how to trigger an Ansible playbook using Python. The playbook is defined in **YAML** format and the inventory file lists the devices that the playbook will interact with.
- The script executes the playbook, retrieves the result, and prints whether the playbook ran successfully or failed.

2. **Integrating Python with SaltStack**:

SaltStack provides a Python API for interacting with its **master** and **minions**. Using the **SaltClient** library, you can execute commands on minions and retrieve the results from within Python scripts.

- **Installation**: To integrate Python with SaltStack, you need to install the `salt` Python library:

bash

```
pip install salt
```

- **Example: Running a Command on a Salt Minion from Python**:

python

185

```python
import salt.client

def     run_salt_command(minion_id,
command):
    # Initialize the Salt client
    client                       =
salt.client.LocalClient()

    # Execute a command on the minion
    result  =  client.cmd(minion_id,
'cmd.run', [command])

    # Print the result
    print(f"Command    output    from
minion {minion_id}: {result}")

# Example usage
run_salt_command('minion1',    'show
version')
```

- o **Explanation**:
  - ▪ The `LocalClient` allows you to interact with SaltStack minions from a Python script. This script sends a **command** (`show version` in this case) to the minion and retrieves the output.

- SaltStack's ability to execute commands across many devices in parallel makes it highly effective for network automation.

Building Automation Workflows Using Python and Ansible

To illustrate the power of combining Python with Ansible, let's create a more complex automation workflow for managing network devices. For example, we can automate the process of updating the hostname and applying basic security configurations to multiple devices in a network.

1. **Step-by-Step Example: Automating Configuration with Ansible and Python**:

   Suppose you need to update the hostname on a series of network devices and configure basic access control lists (ACLs). You can define an Ansible **Playbook** and use Python to trigger it for multiple devices.

   o **Ansible Playbook (update_hostname.yml)**:

   ```yaml

   ---
   ```

```
- name: Update Hostname on Network
Devices
  hosts: all
  tasks:
    - name: Set hostname
      ios_config:
        authorize: yes
        config:
          - hostname "{{ hostname
}}"
    - name: Configure ACL
      ios_config:
        authorize: yes
        config:
          - access-list 100 permit
ip any any
```

o **Python Script to Trigger the Playbook**:

```python
python

import ansible.runner

def
automate_network_config(playbook,
inventory, hostname):
    # Define the options for the
Ansible runner
    options = {
        'playbook': playbook,
```

188

```
        'inventory': inventory,
        'extra_vars': {
            'hostname': hostname   #
Pass    variables    like    hostname
dynamically
        }
    }

    # Execute the playbook
    runner                         =
ansible.runner.Runner(options)
    results = runner.run()

    # Print the results
    if results['status'] == 'ok':
        print(f"Configuration
applied    successfully    on    all
devices.")
    else:
        print(f"Configuration
failed: {results['status']}")

# Example usage
automate_network_config('/path/to/u
pdate_hostname.yml',
'/path/to/inventory', 'Router1')
```

o **Explanation**:

189

- The **Playbook** defines two tasks: one for setting the hostname and another for configuring an access control list (ACL).
- The **Python script** triggers the playbook and passes the desired hostname as a variable (`hostname`).
- By using **Ansible's** `extra_vars`, Python can dynamically pass variables to the playbook, making the automation flexible and scalable.

2. **Managing Configurations on Multiple Devices with Python and Ansible**:

You can expand the Python and Ansible integration by targeting multiple devices in an inventory file. Here's how you can dynamically apply the playbook to multiple devices:

- o **Inventory File (inventory)**:

```ini

[routers]
192.168.1.1
192.168.1.2

[switches]
```

190

```
192.168.2.1
192.168.2.2
```

o **Updated Python Script to Handle Multiple Devices:**

```python
def
automate_network_config_multiple_de
vices(playbook,          inventory,
hostname):
    # Define the options for the
Ansible runner
    options = {
        'playbook': playbook,
        'inventory': inventory,
        'extra_vars': {
            'hostname': hostname   #
Pass   variables   like   hostname
dynamically
        }
    }

    # Execute the playbook
    runner                       =
ansible.runner.Runner(options)
    results = runner.run()
```

191

```
    # Print the results for each
device
    for device, result in
results['contacted'].items():
        if result['status'] == 'ok':
            print(f"Configuration
applied successfully on {device}.")
        else:
            print(f"Failed to apply
configuration on {device}:
{result['status']}")

# Example usage
automate_network_config_multiple_de
vices('/path/to/update_hostname.yml
', '/path/to/inventory', 'Router1')
```

- o **Explanation**:
  - This script allows you to apply the same configuration (hostname and ACL) to multiple devices listed in the **inventory** file, which includes routers and switches.

Conclusion

In this chapter, we've explored how to integrate Python with **Ansible** and **SaltStack** for network automation. By

192

combining Python's flexibility with these powerful configuration management tools, you can automate a wide range of network tasks, from applying configuration changes to collecting and analyzing data. Whether you're working with **Ansible** playbooks or **SaltStack** minions, Python provides a seamless way to trigger automation tasks, manage network configurations, and build sophisticated workflows to improve network reliability and efficiency.

CHAPTER 16

NETWORK DEVICE INVENTORY MANAGEMENT

Automating the Discovery and Inventory Management of Network Devices

In large-scale networks, keeping track of all devices (routers, switches, firewalls, servers, etc.) is critical for efficient management, troubleshooting, and maintenance. Automating the discovery of network devices and their inventory management ensures that network administrators always have an up-to-date record of all devices, which can be easily accessed and audited.

1. **Automating Device Discovery Using Python**

   Device discovery refers to the process of identifying devices connected to a network. Commonly used methods for network device discovery include:

- o **Ping Sweep**: A method for discovering devices by sending ICMP ping requests to a range of IP addresses.
- o **SNMP**: Using the Simple Network Management Protocol to query network devices for their information.
- o **Network Scanning Tools**: Tools like **Nmap** can be used to perform more comprehensive scans of the network.

Python can be used to automate the process of device discovery through a **ping sweep** or **SNMP** queries.

- o **Example: Simple Ping Sweep for Device Discovery**:

```python
python

import subprocess
import ipaddress

def ping_sweep(network):
    # Generate a list of IP addresses
in the network
    network_obj                =
ipaddress.IPv4Network(network)
    reachable_devices = []
```

195

```
for ip in network_obj.hosts():
    response                       =
subprocess.run(['ping', '-c', '1',
str(ip)], stdout=subprocess.PIPE)


    if response.returncode == 0:
# Device is reachable

reachable_devices.append(str(ip))


    return reachable_devices


# Example usage: Discover devices in
the 192.168.1.0/24 network
devices                            =
ping_sweep('192.168.1.0/24')
print(f"Reachable        devices:
{devices}")
```

- o **Explanation**:
  - • The script generates a list of all possible host IP addresses in the given network (192.168.1.0/24) and attempts to ping each IP.
  - • If a device responds, it's added to the list of reachable devices.

196

2. Automating Device Discovery Using SNMP:

- Python's **PySNMP** library can be used to discover devices using SNMP. By querying a well-known SNMP OID (Object Identifier), such as sysDescr, you can gather details about the device, such as its type and version.

```python
from pysnmp.hlapi import *

def discover_device_snmp(ip_address,
community):
    # SNMP OID for system description
    oid = '1.3.6.1.2.1.1.1.0'

    # SNMP GET request
    iterator = getCmd(SnmpEngine(),

CommunityData(community),

UdpTransportTarget((ip_address,
161)),

ContextData(),
```

197

```
ObjectType(ObjectIdentity(oid)))

    error_indication, error_status,
error_index,        var_binds      =
next(iterator)

    if error_indication:
        print(f"Error:
{error_indication}")
    elif error_status:
        print(f"Error        Status:
{error_status.prettyPrint()}")
    else:
        for var_bind in var_binds:
            return var_bind[1]     #
Return the system description (e.g.,
device type)

# Example usage
device_description              =
discover_device_snmp('192.168.1.1',
'public')
print(f"Device        Description:
{device_description}")
```

- **Explanation**:
  - The script queries an SNMP-enabled device for its system

description, which typically contains information about the device type and operating system.

- The response will help identify and catalog devices in the network.

Storing Device Data in a Database or File System

Once devices are discovered, it's crucial to store their data in an accessible format for later use. This data may include device information such as IP address, MAC address, hostname, device type, software version, and more.

1. **Storing Device Data in a File System (CSV)**: Storing device information in a CSV file is a simple way to maintain a record of discovered devices. CSV files can be easily opened with spreadsheet applications and are lightweight for smaller networks.

   o **Example: Storing Device Data in a CSV File**:

   ```python
   ```

```python
import csv

def save_device_inventory(devices,
filename):
    fieldnames = ['IP Address',
'Device Description', 'Hostname']

    with open(filename, mode='w',
newline='') as file:
        writer =
csv.DictWriter(file,
fieldnames=fieldnames)
        writer.writeheader()

        for device in devices:
            writer.writerow(device)

# Example usage
devices = [
    {'IP Address': '192.168.1.1',
'Device Description': 'Cisco IOS',
'Hostname': 'Router1'},
    {'IP Address': '192.168.1.2',
'Device Description': 'Juniper
Junos', 'Hostname': 'Switch1'}
]
save_device_inventory(devices,
'network_inventory.csv')
```

200

- o **Explanation**:
  - The script writes the device data (IP address, description, hostname) to a CSV file called `network_inventory.csv`.
  - CSV format allows you to easily manage and analyze device data.

2. **Storing Device Data in a Database (SQLite)**: For larger networks or more advanced use cases, storing device data in a relational database like **SQLite** allows for better querying and management. Python's **sqlite3** module provides a simple interface for interacting with SQLite databases.

   - o **Example: Storing Device Data in SQLite**:

```python
python

import sqlite3

def    save_device_to_db(device_data,
db_name='network_inventory.db'):
    # Connect to SQLite database (or
create it if it doesn't exist)
    conn = sqlite3.connect(db_name)
    cursor = conn.cursor()

    # Create a table for the network
devices if it doesn't exist
```

```
    cursor.execute('''CREATE    TABLE
IF NOT EXISTS devices
                        (ip_address
TEXT,  description  TEXT,  hostname
TEXT)''')

    # Insert device data into the
table
    cursor.executemany('''INSERT
INTO        devices       (ip_address,
description, hostname)
                             VALUES
(:ip_address,          :description,
:hostname)''', device_data)

    # Commit and close the connection
    conn.commit()
    conn.close()

# Example usage
devices = [
    {'ip_address':    '192.168.1.1',
'description':      'Cisco      IOS',
'hostname': 'Router1'},
    {'ip_address':    '192.168.1.2',
'description':    'Juniper   Junos',
'hostname': 'Switch1'}
]
save_device_to_db(devices)
```

- o **Explanation**:
  - ▪ The script creates an SQLite database (`network_inventory.db`) and stores the device data (IP address, description, hostname) in a `devices` table.
  - ▪ SQLite is lightweight, fast, and doesn't require a separate server, making it a good choice for small to medium-sized networks.

Python Scripts for Generating Device Reports and Audits

Once device data is stored in a file or database, you may want to generate reports or perform audits of the device inventory. These reports could include a list of all devices, an audit of outdated firmware versions, or a list of devices that require configuration updates.

1. **Generating a Simple Inventory Report from a CSV File**: If device data is stored in a CSV file, you can write a Python script to generate a simple inventory report.

   - o **Example: Generating a Report from a CSV Inventory**:

```python

import csv

def
generate_inventory_report(filename)
:
    with open(filename, mode='r') as
file:
        reader                       =
csv.DictReader(file)
        print(f"Network        Device
Inventory Report:")
        print(f"{'IP
Address':<20}{'Device
Description':<25}{'Hostname':<20}")
        print("-" * 65)

        for row in reader:
            print(f"{row['IP
Address']:<20}{row['Device
Description']:<25}{row['Hostname']:
<20}")

# Example usage
generate_inventory_report('network_
inventory.csv')
```

- o **Explanation**:

- The script reads the CSV file (`network_inventory.csv`), processes each row, and prints a formatted report that lists all the devices.

2. **Generating an Audit Report from SQLite Database**: You can query the SQLite database to generate more complex reports, such as devices with a specific firmware version or devices that need updates.

   o **Example: Generating an Audit Report from SQLite**:

```python
import sqlite3

def
generate_audit_report(db_name='netw
ork_inventory.db'):
    # Connect to SQLite database
    conn = sqlite3.connect(db_name)
    cursor = conn.cursor()

    # Query devices that need
firmware updates (example)
    cursor.execute('''SELECT
ip_address, description, hostname
```

205

```
                    FROM    devices
WHERE        description        LIKE
'%old_version%''''')

    devices_to_update          =
cursor.fetchall()

    # Print audit report
    print(f"Audit   Report:   Devices
with outdated firmware")
    print(f"{'IP
Address':<20}{'Device
Description':<25}{'Hostname':<20}")
    print("-" * 65)

    for device in devices_to_update:

print(f"{device[0]:<20}{device[1]:<
25}{device[2]:<20}")

    # Close the connection
    conn.close()

# Example usage
generate_audit_report()
```

o **Explanation**:

  ▪ The script queries the SQLite database
    for devices with outdated firmware and

206

generates a report with IP addresses, descriptions, and hostnames of devices that need updates.

In this chapter, we've covered the automation of **network device discovery** using Python, methods for storing device data in a file system (CSV) or a database (SQLite), and generating device reports and audits. By automating inventory management and using Python for reporting, network administrators can save time, reduce human error, and keep their networks organized. These practices help ensure that network devices are tracked, managed, and updated efficiently, promoting better network performance and security. In the next chapter, we will explore how to integrate these automation tasks with larger network management platforms for even more scalable solutions.

CHAPTER 17

WORKING WITH NETWORK TOPOLOGY

Automating Network Topology Discovery

Network topology discovery is an essential task in network management. It helps network administrators understand how devices are interconnected and identify potential bottlenecks, security vulnerabilities, or points of failure. Automating the discovery of network topology allows for real-time updates and accurate mapping of network devices, simplifying management, troubleshooting, and optimization.

1. **Automating Discovery with SNMP and LLDP (Link Layer Discovery Protocol):** Many modern network devices support protocols like **SNMP** and **LLDP** for discovering network topology. **SNMP** provides detailed device information such as interfaces, IP addresses, and device types, while **LLDP** allows devices to advertise information about their neighbors in the network.

o **Using SNMP for Topology Discovery**: Python's **PySNMP** library can query network devices for topology-related data, such as interface status and connectivity details.

```python
from pysnmp.hlapi import *
import json

def discover_topology(ip_address, community):
    # SNMP OIDs for discovering interface and neighbors (using LLDP)
    interface_oid = '1.3.6.1.2.1.2.2.1.2'  # Interface name OID
    lldp_neighbors_oid = '1.0.8802.1.1.2.1.4.1.1.9'  # LLDP neighbors OID

    iterator = getCmd(SnmpEngine(),

CommunityData(community),

UdpTransportTarget((ip_address, 161)),

ContextData(),
```

209

```
ObjectType(ObjectIdentity(interface
_oid)),

ObjectType(ObjectIdentity(lldp_neig
hbors_oid)))

    error_indication, error_status,
error_index,       var_binds       =
next(iterator)

    if error_indication:
        print(f"Error:
{error_indication}")
    elif error_status:
        print(f"Error       Status:
{error_status.prettyPrint()}")
    else:
        topology_data = {}
        for var_bind in var_binds:
            # Extract interface and
neighbor information
            device_info           =
var_bind[1]

topology_data[str(var_bind[0])]    =
str(device_info)

        return topology_data
```

210

```
# Example usage
topology                        =
discover_topology('192.168.1.1',
'public')
print(json.dumps(topology,
indent=2))
```

- o **Explanation**:
  - The script uses **SNMP** to query a network device for interface and neighbor information.
  - The topology data, such as interface names and LLDP neighbor information, is collected and printed as a JSON object.
  - This data can then be used to map the topology or trigger further actions based on connectivity details.

2. **Using Nmap for Network Topology Discovery**: **Nmap** is a powerful network scanning tool that can be used to discover devices, open ports, and map the network topology. Python's **python-nmap** library allows you to integrate Nmap with Python to automate network discovery.

   - o **Installation**:

     ```
     bash
     ```

211

```
pip install python-nmap
```

o **Example: Using Nmap for Network Topology Discovery**:

```python
import nmap

def
discover_network_topology(network_r
ange):
    # Initialize the Nmap scanner
    nm = nmap.PortScanner()

    # Scan the specified network
range
    nm.scan(hosts=network_range,
arguments='-sn')    # Ping scan (no
port scanning)

    topology_data = {}

    for host in nm.all_hosts():
        topology_data[host] = {
            'hostname':
nm[host].hostname(),
```

212

```
                    'status':
nm[host].state(),
                      'os':
nm[host].os_fingerprint()
                        }


        return topology_data


# Example usage
topology                        =
discover_network_topology('192.168.
1.0/24')
print(topology)
```

- o **Explanation**:
  - The script uses **Nmap** to perform a **ping scan** (-sn) over the network range (192.168.1.0/24).
  - The results are stored in a dictionary with information about each host, including its **hostname, status**, and **OS fingerprint**.

Using Python to Visualize Network Topology

Visualizing the network topology is an important step in understanding network architecture, detecting vulnerabilities, and optimizing performance. Python, in

213

combination with libraries like **NetworkX** and **Matplotlib**, can be used to create visual representations of the network topology.

1. **Visualizing Topology with NetworkX and Matplotlib**: NetworkX is a Python library for the creation, manipulation, and study of the structure and dynamics of complex networks. It can be used to model network topologies as graphs, where devices are nodes, and connections are edges.

   o **Installation**:

   ```bash
   bash
   ```

   ```bash
   pip install networkx matplotlib
   ```

   o **Example: Visualizing a Simple Network Topology**:

   ```python
   python
   ```

   ```python
   import networkx as nx
   import matplotlib.pyplot as plt

   def
   visualize_network_topology(devices)
   :
   ```

214

```
    G = nx.Graph()  # Create an empty
graph

    # Add nodes (devices) to the
graph
    for device in devices:

G.add_node(device['hostname'],
ip=device['ip'])

    # Add edges (connections between
devices)
    for connection in devices:
        for neighbor in
connection.get('neighbors', []):

G.add_edge(connection['hostname'],
neighbor)

    # Draw the network topology
    pos = nx.spring_layout(G)
    nx.draw(G,                  pos,
with_labels=True,    node_size=2000,
node_color='skyblue',  font_size=10,
font_weight='bold',
edge_color='gray')
    plt.show()

# Example usage
```

```
devices = [
    {'hostname': 'Router1', 'ip':
'192.168.1.1', 'neighbors':
['Switch1']},
    {'hostname': 'Switch1', 'ip':
'192.168.1.2', 'neighbors':
['Router1', 'PC1']},
    {'hostname': 'PC1', 'ip':
'192.168.1.3', 'neighbors':
['Switch1']}
]
visualize_network_topology(devices)
```

o **Explanation**:

■ The script uses **NetworkX** to create a graph representing devices as nodes and their connections as edges.

■ **Matplotlib** is used to visualize the graph, where each node represents a network device (e.g., router, switch, PC).

■ The layout of the graph is determined using **spring_layout**, which arranges nodes in a visually appealing way.

2. **Visualizing Topology from SNMP or Nmap Data**: Once you have collected topology data using SNMP or Nmap, you can visualize it by converting the collected data into nodes and edges.

216

- o **Example: Visualizing Topology from SNMP Data**:

```python
def
visualize_snmp_topology(ip_addresse
s):
    devices = [{'hostname': ip,
'ip': ip, 'neighbors': []} for ip in
ip_addresses]

    # Simulate neighbors for
demonstration
devices[0]['neighbors'].append(devi
ces[1]['hostname'])

devices[1]['neighbors'].append(devi
ces[2]['hostname'])


visualize_network_topology(devices)

# Example usage with discovered IPs
visualize_snmp_topology(['192.168.1
.1', '192.168.1.2', '192.168.1.3'])
```

- o **Explanation**:

217

- This example shows how to visualize topology based on SNMP-discovered devices. Each device is represented as a node, and connections (neighbors) are represented as edges.

Integration with Third-Party Tools for Topology Management

For large-scale networks, integrating Python with third-party topology management tools can help streamline network monitoring, configuration, and optimization. Some commonly used tools for managing network topology include **SolarWinds Network Topology Mapper**, **NetBox**, and **PRTG Network Monitor**.

1. **Integrating Python with NetBox for Topology Management**: **NetBox** is an open-source IP address management (IPAM) and data center infrastructure management (DCIM) tool that includes topology management features. NetBox exposes a REST API that allows Python to automate the creation, retrieval, and management of network devices and their relationships.

   o **Installation**:

218

```bash
bash

pip install pynetbox
```

o **Example: Interacting with NetBox via Python API**:

```python
python

import pynetbox

def get_device_topology():
    netbox_url    =    'http://your-netbox-url/api/'
    token = 'your-netbox-token'

    # Connect to NetBox API
    nb = pynetbox.api(netbox_url)
    nb.token = token

    # Fetch devices from NetBox
    devices = nb.dcim.devices.all()

    # Print device topology information
    for device in devices:
        print(f"Device: {device.name},             IP: {device.primary_ip4}")
```

219

```
get_device_topology()
```

○ **Explanation**:

- The script connects to the **NetBox** API and fetches a list of devices from the data center infrastructure.
- You can use this data to build a more detailed and interactive topology map by integrating Python scripts with NetBox.

2. **Using APIs for Third-Party Topology Tools**: Similarly, you can use APIs from other third-party topology tools like **PRTG Network Monitor** or **SolarWinds Network Topology Mapper** to fetch and manage network topology data. Python scripts can automate interactions with these APIs, allowing for seamless integration into network monitoring and management workflows.

In this chapter, we explored how to automate the discovery of network topology, visualize the topology using Python, and integrate with third-party tools for topology management. By automating topology discovery and using visualization techniques, network administrators can gain

220

valuable insights into their network's architecture, optimize performance, and proactively address potential issues. In the next chapter, we will discuss advanced network automation techniques, including integrating machine learning for predictive analysis and optimization.

CHAPTER 18

INTEGRATING PYTHON WITH CLOUD NETWORKING

Introduction to Cloud Networking (AWS, Azure, Google Cloud)

Cloud networking involves the use of cloud computing resources to host and manage network infrastructure, services, and resources. Major cloud providers such as **Amazon Web Services (AWS)**, **Microsoft Azure**, and **Google Cloud Platform (GCP)** offer a variety of cloud networking services that allow users to create, manage, and scale virtual networks, load balancers, firewalls, and other network-related services.

These platforms enable businesses to move away from traditional on-premise networking, offering scalable, flexible, and cost-efficient solutions. Python plays a significant role in cloud networking automation by enabling the management and configuration of cloud resources via APIs, allowing developers and network administrators to automate tasks, such as provisioning cloud resources, configuring networks, and managing security.

1. **Amazon Web Services (AWS)**:
   - AWS provides a comprehensive suite of cloud networking services, including **Virtual Private Cloud (VPC), Elastic Load Balancing (ELB), Route 53** (DNS service), and more. These services help users build scalable and secure networks in the cloud.
   - AWS provides an SDK called **Boto3**, which allows Python to interact with AWS services, making it easier to automate cloud networking tasks.

2. **Microsoft Azure**:
   - Azure offers a range of networking services, including **Azure Virtual Network, Load Balancer, Application Gateway**, and **Azure DNS**. With Azure, users can easily create and manage virtual networks, secure their applications, and integrate with on-premise systems.
   - Azure provides a Python SDK called **azure-sdk-for-python**, which facilitates integration with Azure services for automation and management.

3. **Google Cloud Platform (GCP)**:

- o GCP provides networking services like **Virtual Private Cloud (VPC)**, **Cloud Load Balancing**, **Cloud DNS**, and **Firewall Rules**. Google Cloud networking services allow users to build, scale, and secure their network infrastructure in the cloud.
- o Google provides the **google-cloud-python** SDK, which offers Python bindings for interacting with GCP services, enabling network automation in the cloud.

Automating Cloud Network Configurations and Administration Tasks

Python can be used to automate various tasks related to cloud network configurations and administration, such as setting up virtual networks, managing IP addressing, configuring firewalls, and provisioning virtual machines. Below are some real-world examples of how Python can be used to automate cloud networking tasks across AWS, Azure, and GCP.

1. **Automating Network Configuration in AWS Using Python (Boto3)**

In AWS, **Boto3** is the official Python SDK that allows you to interact with AWS services. You can use Boto3 to automate network configuration tasks like creating a **VPC**, setting up **subnets**, and configuring **security groups**.

- o **Example: Creating a VPC in AWS using Boto3**:

```python
python

import boto3

def create_vpc():
    ec2 = boto3.client('ec2')

    # Create a VPC
    vpc_response = ec2.create_vpc(CidrBlock='10.0.0.0/16')
    vpc_id = vpc_response['Vpc']['VpcId']

    # Enable DNS support and DNS hostnames

    ec2.modify_vpc_attribute(VpcId=vpc_
```

225

```
id,        EnableDnsSupport={'Value':
True})

ec2.modify_vpc_attribute(VpcId=vpc_
id,        EnableDnsHostnames={'Value':
True})

    print(f"VPC    created    with    ID:
{vpc_id}")

    return vpc_id

create_vpc()
```

- o **Explanation**:
  - The script uses **Boto3** to create a **VPC** with the CIDR block `10.0.0.0/16`.
  - It then enables DNS support and DNS hostnames for the VPC.
  - This type of automation helps quickly provision network resources on AWS.

2. **Automating Network Configuration in Azure Using Python (azure-sdk-for-python)**

Azure offers a Python SDK that allows you to interact with Azure networking services. You can automate tasks like creating a **Virtual Network**, managing **subnets**, and configuring **network security groups** (NSGs).

- o **Example: Creating a Virtual Network in Azure**:

```python
from azure.identity import DefaultAzureCredential
from azure.mgmt.network import NetworkManagementClient

def create_virtual_network():
    credential = DefaultAzureCredential()
    subscription_id = 'your_subscription_id'
    network_client = NetworkManagementClient(credential, subscription_id)

    # Create a virtual network
    vnet_name = "MyVNet"
    resource_group_name = "MyResourceGroup"
    location = "East US"

    vnet_params = {
```

227

```
    "location": location,
    "address_space":
{"address_prefixes":
["10.0.0.0/16"]}
    }


    vnet                         =
network_client.virtual_networks.beg
in_create_or_update(
        resource_group_name,
vnet_name, vnet_params
    ).result()


    print(f"Virtual Network created:
{vnet.name}")


create_virtual_network()
```

- o **Explanation**:
  - ▪ The script uses **azure-sdk-for-python** to authenticate and interact with Azure's network management services.
  - ▪ It creates a virtual network with the address prefix `10.0.0.0/16` in the specified resource group and location.

3. **Automating Network Configuration in Google Cloud Using Python (google-cloud-python)**

228

Google Cloud offers powerful networking services like **VPC, Cloud Load Balancer**, and **Firewall Rules**. You can automate tasks such as creating VPCs, setting up firewall rules, and managing IP ranges with **google-cloud-python**.

- o **Example: Creating a VPC in Google Cloud**:

```python
python

from google.cloud import compute_v1
from        google.oauth2        import
service_account

def create_vpc():
    credentials                      =
service_account.Credentials.from_se
rvice_account_file(
        'your-service-account-
key.json'
    )

    client                           =
compute_v1.NetworksClient(credentia
ls=credentials)
    project = 'your-project-id'
    region = 'us-central1'
```

```
# Create VPC
network = compute_v1.Network()
network.name = 'my-vpc'
network.auto_create_subnetworks
= False

    operation                    =
client.insert(project=project,
region=region,
network_resource=network)
    operation.result()

    print(f"VPC 'my-vpc' created in
{region}")

create_vpc()
```

- o **Explanation**:
  - ▪ The script uses the **google-cloud-python** SDK to create a VPC in Google Cloud.
  - ▪ It uses the `insert` method to add a new VPC with the name `'my-vpc'` and disables the auto-creation of subnets.
  - ▪ This automation can be extended to include subnet creation and other networking tasks.

230

Real-World Use Cases of Python in Cloud Networking Automation

Python is widely used in real-world cloud networking automation due to its flexibility, ease of integration, and support for cloud provider SDKs. Below are several use cases where Python can automate cloud networking tasks:

1. **Automating Cloud Infrastructure Deployment:** Many organizations use Python to automatically deploy cloud infrastructure, including virtual networks, VMs, firewalls, and load balancers. For example, Python can be used to create a new VPC, deploy subnets, configure routing tables, and set up network security rules for a new application environment.

   o **Use Case Example**: Automating the deployment of a new multi-tier web application with VPC, subnets, and security groups in AWS.

2. **Automating Cloud Network Monitoring and Alerts:** Python can be used to automate the collection of network performance metrics from cloud networking services, such as monitoring the traffic of a virtual private cloud (VPC) in AWS or a virtual network in Azure. Python can also be

integrated with cloud monitoring tools like **CloudWatch** (AWS), **Azure Monitor**, or **Stackdriver** (GCP) to send real-time alerts based on predefined thresholds.

- o **Use Case Example**: Automating the creation of CloudWatch alarms in AWS to notify administrators if network traffic exceeds certain thresholds or if there is an unusual spike in data transfers.

3. **Automating Cloud Network Security Configurations:** Python can be used to automate the configuration of network security, such as applying firewall rules, managing **Network Access Control Lists (NACLs)**, and configuring **Security Groups** in AWS, Azure, or GCP. Security configurations can be automated based on best practices or the specific requirements of the environment.

- o **Use Case Example**: Automating the process of setting up firewall rules for a multi-cloud architecture, ensuring that all virtual machines are properly secured with the correct ingress and egress rules.

4. **Provisioning Load Balancers and Network Routes:** Python scripts can automate the provisioning of load balancers and the configuration

of routing tables for traffic distribution across multiple regions or availability zones in a cloud environment.

- o **Use Case Example**: Using Python to provision an **Elastic Load Balancer (ELB)** in AWS or a **Google Cloud Load Balancer**, and configure its associated routing rules to distribute traffic evenly.

Conclusion

In this chapter, we've explored how Python can be used to automate cloud networking tasks in **AWS**, **Azure**, and **Google Cloud**, including configuring virtual networks, provisioning load balancers, and managing firewalls. By using the cloud provider's Python SDKs, network administrators can automate many aspects of cloud networking, improving efficiency, scalability, and consistency. Whether deploying new infrastructure, automating network monitoring, or configuring security rules, Python provides the flexibility to integrate seamlessly into cloud networking environments. This automation is a crucial component of modern cloud operations and can significantly reduce the overhead of manual configuration and management tasks.

CHAPTER 19

AUTOMATION FOR NETWORK PERFORMANCE TUNING

Using Python to Automatically Adjust Network Settings Based on Performance Metrics

Network performance is crucial for maintaining the reliability and efficiency of modern networks. Factors like **latency**, **bandwidth utilization**, **packet loss**, and **jitter** directly impact the quality of service (QoS) provided to users and applications. With the help of Python, network administrators can automate the collection of performance metrics, analyze the data, and make real-time adjustments to network settings based on performance indicators.

1. **Automating Network Performance Metrics Collection:**

Python can be used to gather network performance metrics such as bandwidth utilization, latency, and packet loss using a variety of methods, such as SNMP queries, **ping** tests, or leveraging third-party network monitoring tools like **Nagios**, **Prometheus**, or **Zabbix**.

- o **Example: Automating Network Performance Monitoring Using SNMP**:

```python
python

from pysnmp.hlapi import *
import time

def get_network_traffic(ip_address,
community):
    # OID for incoming traffic
(ifInOctets) and outgoing traffic
(ifOutOctets)
    incoming_traffic_oid       =
'1.3.6.1.2.1.2.2.1.10'
    outgoing_traffic_oid       =
'1.3.6.1.2.1.2.2.1.16'

    iterator = getCmd(SnmpEngine(),

CommunityData(community),
```

```
UdpTransportTarget((ip_address,
161)),

ContextData(),

ObjectType(ObjectIdentity(incoming_
traffic_oid)),

ObjectType(ObjectIdentity(outgoing_
traffic_oid)))

    error_indication,  error_status,
error_index,       var_binds      =
next(iterator)

    if error_indication:
        print(f"Error:
{error_indication}")
    elif error_status:
        print(f"Error       Status:
{error_status.prettyPrint()}")
    else:
        traffic_data = {}
        for var_bind in var_binds:

traffic_data[str(var_bind[0])]      =
var_bind[1]
        return traffic_data
```

```
# Example usage
traffic                    =
get_network_traffic('192.168.1.1',
'public')
print(f"Network Traffic: {traffic}")
```

- o **Explanation**:
  - The script uses **SNMP** to query a network device for its incoming and outgoing traffic statistics.
  - These metrics can help assess whether the network is operating within acceptable performance thresholds and guide any necessary adjustments.

2. **Using Performance Metrics to Adjust Network Settings:**

Once network performance metrics are collected, Python can be used to automatically adjust network settings based on predefined performance thresholds. For example, if **bandwidth utilization** exceeds a certain threshold, Python can automatically adjust the **QoS** or **routing parameters** to prioritize critical traffic.

o **Example: Automatically Adjusting Bandwidth Utilization**:

```python
import subprocess

def adjust_bandwidth(ip_address, threshold=80):
    # Example: Ping test to measure bandwidth utilization
    result = subprocess.run(['ping', '-c', '4', ip_address], stdout=subprocess.PIPE)

    # Simulated logic: If average latency exceeds threshold, adjust network settings
    if result.returncode == 0:
        output = result.stdout.decode('utf-8')
        average_latency = float(output.split('=')[-1].split('/')[1])
        print(f"Average latency: {average_latency} ms")

        if average_latency > threshold:
```

238

```
            print("Adjusting        QoS
settings    to    prioritize    critical
traffic.")
            # Implement  commands  to
adjust QoS, routing, etc.
    else:
        print(f"Failed    to    ping
{ip_address}")


# Example usage
adjust_bandwidth('192.168.1.1')
```

- o **Explanation**:
  - The script pings a device to measure **latency**.
  - If the average latency exceeds a predefined threshold, the script can trigger actions such as adjusting **QoS settings** or modifying **routing protocols** to optimize network performance.

Automating Quality of Service (QoS) Adjustments

Quality of Service (QoS) is a critical feature for managing network traffic, ensuring that high-priority traffic (e.g., voice, video, or critical applications) receives preferential treatment, while less time-sensitive traffic (e.g., file downloads, bulk data transfers) is deprioritized. Python can automate QoS adjustments to optimize network performance based on real-time data.

1. **Automating QoS Configuration on Network Devices**:

   Python can be used to configure **QoS policies** on network devices (e.g., Cisco routers) using **Netmiko**, which allows remote configuration via SSH.

   o **Example: Automating QoS Configuration Using Netmiko (Cisco Router)**:

   ```python
   from netmiko import ConnectHandler

   def configure_qos(ip_address, username, password):
       device = {
           'device_type': 'cisco_ios',
           'host': ip_address,
           'username': username,
           'password': password,
       }

       try:
   ```

240

```python
    # Connect to the device
    net_connect                =
ConnectHandler(**device)
    net_connect.enable()

    # Configure QoS settings:
Priority queue for VoIP
    qos_config = [
        'class-map      match-any
VoIP',
        'match ip dscp ef',   #
DSCP   value   for   EF   (Expedited
Forwarding) for VoIP
        'policy-map QoS-Policy',
        'class VoIP',
        'priority   512',        #
Reserve bandwidth for VoIP traffic
        'interface
GigabitEthernet0/1',
        'service-policy   output
QoS-Policy'
    ]

    # Apply QoS configuration

net_connect.send_config_set(qos_con
fig)
    print("QoS      configuration
applied successfully.")
```

```
        #        Disconnect        after
configuration
        net_connect.disconnect()

    except Exception as e:
        print(f"Error        configuring
QoS on {ip_address}: {e}")

# Example usage
configure_qos('192.168.1.1',
'admin', 'password')
```

o **Explanation**:

- The script connects to a **Cisco device** using **Netmiko** and applies a QoS configuration.

- It prioritizes **VoIP** traffic by configuring a **class-map** and **policy-map** to ensure VoIP packets are treated with priority and reserved bandwidth.

- This type of automation allows administrators to optimize network performance for latency-sensitive applications like voice and video.

2. **Automating QoS Adjustments Based on Traffic Patterns**:

242

In a dynamic environment, QoS adjustments may need to be made in real time based on changing traffic patterns. Python can be used to monitor network traffic and dynamically adjust QoS settings as needed.

- o **Example: Dynamically Adjusting QoS Based on Traffic Load**:

```python
python

def
dynamic_qos_adjustment(ip_address,
traffic_threshold=70):
    # Example: Monitor traffic
metrics (simulated)
    traffic_load            =
get_network_traffic(ip_address)   #
Use previous methods to get traffic

    if
traffic_load['incoming_traffic']   >
traffic_threshold:
        print("High           traffic
detected.   Adjusting   QoS   to
prioritize critical traffic.")
```

243

```
        configure_qos(ip_address,
'admin', 'password')    # Apply QoS
configuration
    else:
        print("Traffic    is    within
normal limits. No QoS adjustments
needed.")

# Example usage
dynamic_qos_adjustment('192.168.1.1
')
```

- o **Explanation**:
  - The script monitors the **incoming traffic load** on a network device. If the load exceeds a threshold (e.g., 70%), it triggers the QoS configuration to prioritize critical traffic.
  - This dynamic approach ensures that the network is always optimized based on real-time performance data.

Ensuring Network Stability Through Automated Performance Optimization

Network stability is essential for ensuring continuous service availability and minimizing disruptions. Python can automate network performance optimization tasks to proactively identify and resolve performance bottlenecks before they impact users.

1. **Automating Network Troubleshooting and Optimization**:

   Python can automate tasks such as **pinging** devices, **tracerouting**, or checking **interface status** to identify performance issues like **latency**, **packet loss**, or **congestion**. Based on the results, Python can trigger corrective actions like **load balancing** or **rerouting** traffic.

   o **Example: Automating Latency and Packet Loss Troubleshooting**:

   ```python
   python

   import subprocess

   def
   troubleshoot_network(ip_address):
       # Ping the device to check for
   latency and packet loss
       result = subprocess.run(['ping',
   '-c',        '4',        ip_address],
   ```

```python
                            stdout=subprocess.PIPE,
                            stderr=subprocess.PIPE)

    if result.returncode == 0:
        output                   =
result.stdout.decode('utf-8')
        packet_loss              =
output.split('packet
loss')[0].split()[-2]
        average_latency          =
float(output.split('=')[-
1].split('/')[1])


        print(f"Packet            Loss:
{packet_loss}%")
        print(f"Average      Latency:
{average_latency} ms")


        if float(packet_loss) > 10:
            print("Packet          loss
detected. Rerouting traffic.")
            #    Implement    traffic
rerouting logic here
        elif average_latency > 100:
            print("High          latency
detected.    Adjusting    QoS    or
rerouting.")
            #       Implement      QoS
adjustments or rerouting logic here
```

246

```
    else:
        print(f"Failed    to    ping
{ip_address}")

# Example usage
troubleshoot_network('192.168.1.1')
```

- o **Explanation**:
  - The script checks **packet loss** and **latency** by pinging a device and analyzing the results.
  - If packet loss exceeds a threshold (e.g., 10%), the script can automatically trigger actions such as rerouting traffic or adjusting QoS to improve performance.

2. **Proactive Network Optimization**:

Proactive network optimization focuses on continuously monitoring network performance, identifying bottlenecks, and adjusting settings before issues impact network stability.

- o **Example: Proactive Network Optimization**:

```
python
```

```
def
proactive_network_optimization(ip_a
ddress):
    # Continuously monitor network
performance metrics
    while True:
        traffic_data              =
get_network_traffic(ip_address)
        if
traffic_data['incoming_traffic']   >
80:    #  Traffic  exceeds  80%  of
capacity
            print("High       traffic
detected.      Adjusting      bandwidth
allocation.")

adjust_bandwidth(ip_address)
            time.sleep(300)    #  Wait  5
minutes before checking again

proactive_network_optimization('192
.168.1.1')
```

- o **Explanation**:
  - The script continuously monitors network traffic every 5 minutes and adjusts bandwidth allocation or other performance parameters if the traffic exceeds a defined threshold.

248

Conclusion

In this chapter, we've explored how Python can be used for **network performance tuning**, from automatically adjusting network settings based on performance metrics to automating **QoS adjustments** and ensuring network stability through proactive optimization. By automating performance monitoring and adjustments, network administrators can ensure that their networks run efficiently, minimizing downtime and optimizing performance for critical applications. This level of automation allows for a more responsive and adaptive network environment, ensuring optimal user experiences and seamless operations.

4o mini

CHAPTER 20

BUILDING CUSTOM NETWORK AUTOMATION TOOLS

Creating Custom Python Tools for Specific Network Tasks

In network automation, creating custom Python tools tailored to your organization's unique needs can significantly enhance operational efficiency. By building Python tools, you can automate repetitive tasks, customize solutions for specific use cases, and streamline workflows. Python's flexibility and robust libraries make it an ideal language for developing custom network automation tools.

1. **Identifying Network Automation Needs:** Before creating a custom tool, it's important to identify the network automation tasks that need automation. Some common use cases include:

   o **Network Configuration Management**: Automating backup, configuration, and restoration of network devices.

- o **Performance Monitoring**: Automatically collecting and analyzing metrics like bandwidth usage, latency, and packet loss.
- o **Network Troubleshooting**: Building tools to run diagnostics such as ping tests, traceroutes, and interface status checks.

2. **Custom Python Tool for Network Configuration Backup:**

A common network task is backing up configurations of network devices. A custom tool can be built to automate this process using Python and libraries like **Netmiko**.

- o **Example: Custom Python Tool for Backing Up Cisco Router Configurations**:

```python
python

from netmiko import ConnectHandler
import time
import os

def
backup_router_configuration(ip_addr
ess,        username,        password,
backup_dir):
    device = {
```

```
        'device_type': 'cisco_ios',
        'host': ip_address,
        'username': username,
        'password': password,
        'secret':   password,      #
Enable password
    }

    try:
        # Establish SSH connection
to the device
        net_connect              =
ConnectHandler(**device)
        net_connect.enable()

        #    Retrieve   the   running
configuration
        config                   =
net_connect.send_command('show
running-config')

        # Save the configuration to
a backup file
        timestamp                =
time.strftime("%Y%m%d-%H%M%S")
        backup_filename          =
os.path.join(backup_dir,
f"config_backup_{ip_address}_{times
tamp}.txt")
```

```
        with    open(backup_filename,
'w') as backup_file:

backup_file.write(config)

        print(f"Configuration backup
saved to {backup_filename}")
        net_connect.disconnect()

    except Exception as e:
        print(f"Error    backing    up
configuration    from    {ip_address}:
{e}")

# Example usage
backup_router_configuration('192.16
8.1.1',      'admin',      'password',
'/path/to/backups')
```

- o **Explanation**:
  - This script uses **Netmiko** to connect to a Cisco router, retrieve the running configuration, and save it to a timestamped backup file.
  - This tool can be customized to support other device types or even be extended to

253

include   configuration   restoration capabilities.

Packaging and Distributing Python Automation Tools

Once your custom Python tool is developed and tested, it's time to package it and distribute it for use within your network team or organization. Python tools can be packaged and shared easily, allowing other administrators to run the tool on different systems without requiring them to manually install dependencies.

1. **Creating a Python Package for Distribution**: Python's **setuptools** library is a great tool for packaging Python scripts into distributable formats like .tar.gz or .whl (wheel files). This allows your tools to be installed via **pip**.

   o **Example: Creating a Python Package**:

     1. **Project Structure**:

```arduino
network_automation_tool/
├── network_automation_tool/
│   └── __init__.py
│   └── backup_tool.py
```

```
├── setup.py
├── README.md
└── requirements.txt
```

2. **setup.py** (setup script for packaging):

python

```python
from setuptools import setup,
find_packages

setup(

name='network_automation_tool
',
    version='1.0.0',
    description='A custom tool
for      automating      network
tasks.',
    author='Your Name',

author_email='your.email@exam
ple.com',
    packages=find_packages(),
    install_requires=[
        'netmiko',
        'paramiko',
        'pysnmp',
    ],
    entry_points={
```

255

```
'console_scripts': [
        'network-
backup=network_automation_too
l.backup_tool:main',
        ],
    },
)
```

3. **README.md** (documentation for users):

```
markdown

# Network Automation Tool

A simple tool for automating network backup tasks.

## Installation

To install the tool, run:

```bash
pip                        install
network_automation_tool
```

Usage

Use the `network-backup` command to back up network configurations:
```

```
bash
```

```
network-backup          --ip
192.168.1.1 --username admin -
-password  password  --backup-
dir /path/to/backups
```

4. **Creating a Distribution**: Once your code is ready, run the following command to create a distributable package:

```
bash
```

```
python     setup.py     sdist
bdist_wheel
```

5. **Installing the Package**: After building the package, you can install it using pip:

```
bash
```

```
pip                  install
dist/network_automation_tool-
1.0.0.tar.gz
```

2. **Distributing the Package**:

- o **PyPI (Python Package Index)**: You can upload the package to PyPI to make it publicly available to everyone. This involves registering an account on PyPI, creating a ~/.pypirc configuration file, and running:

```bash
twine upload dist/*
```

- o **Private Repository**: If your tool is for internal use, you can host it on a private **PyPI server** or use **GitHub** to distribute the source code.

3. **Creating Command-Line Tools**: Python packages can be integrated with command-line interfaces (CLI) using **argparse** or by defining **entry points** in the setup.py. This allows users to run the tool directly from the terminal.

- o **Example: Adding CLI to the Backup Tool**:

```python
import argparse

def main():
    parser                         =
argparse.ArgumentParser(description
="Network Backup Tool")
```

258

```
    parser.add_argument('--ip',
required=True,     help="Device     IP
address")
    parser.add_argument('--
username',               required=True,
help="Device username")
    parser.add_argument('--
password',               required=True,
help="Device password")
    parser.add_argument('--backup-
dir', required=True, help="Directory
for backup files")

    args = parser.parse_args()

    # Call the backup function

backup_router_configuration(args.ip
,   args.username,   args.password,
args.backup_dir)

if __name__ == "__main__":
    main()
```

- o **Explanation**:
  - This script enables the tool to be run from the command line with various options like --ip, --username, --password, and --backup-dir.

259

- Once the package is installed, users can invoke the tool using the command `network-backup`.

Real-World Examples of Custom Tools for Automation

1. **Automated Network Configuration Backup Tool**:
   - o **Use Case**: Automatically backing up configurations from routers, switches, and firewalls at regular intervals.
   - o **Implementation**: A Python script using **Netmiko** and **Paramiko** to SSH into network devices, retrieve the configuration, and store it securely in a cloud or local storage.

2. **Bandwidth Monitoring Tool**:
   - o **Use Case**: Monitoring network traffic and generating alerts when bandwidth utilization exceeds a threshold.
   - o **Implementation**: Python can be used to periodically check network traffic using SNMP or **Nmap**, analyze bandwidth usage, and trigger alerts via email or text message if thresholds are exceeded.

3. **Network Health Monitoring Dashboard**:

260

- o **Use Case**: A web-based dashboard displaying real-time network health statistics like latency, packet loss, and uptime for all devices.
- o **Implementation**: Python with **Flask** or **Django** can be used to create a web application, while libraries like **psutil** and **Matplotlib** can be used to monitor and visualize network metrics.

4. **Automated Firewall Rules Configuration**:
   - o **Use Case**: Automatically configuring firewall rules based on traffic patterns or security events.
   - o **Implementation**: Python scripts that interact with **Firewall APIs** (such as **Palo Alto Networks**, **Cisco ASA**, or **Juniper SRX**) to dynamically adjust firewall rules based on network traffic analysis.

Conclusion

In this chapter, we've explored how to build custom Python tools for specific network tasks, such as configuration backups, bandwidth monitoring, and firewall management. By automating routine network tasks, custom Python tools can help network administrators improve efficiency, reduce errors, and ensure consistent network management. Additionally, we covered how to package and distribute these tools using Python's `setuptools`, making them easy to share with others. The flexibility of Python allows you to develop tailored solutions to meet the unique requirements of your network, making it an invaluable tool for network automation.

CHAPTER 21

NETWORK AUTOMATION AND DEVOPS

Introduction to DevOps in Network Management

DevOps, a combination of "Development" and "Operations," is a set of practices aimed at automating and integrating the processes of software development and IT operations. DevOps emphasizes collaboration, continuous integration, and continuous delivery (CI/CD) to achieve faster, more efficient software development cycles. In network management, DevOps practices can be applied to automate network provisioning, monitoring, configuration management, and troubleshooting, ultimately improving network performance and reducing manual intervention.

The integration of **DevOps** in network management allows teams to automate repetitive tasks, enforce consistent network configurations, and implement faster deployments of network services. Through tools like **Ansible**, **Terraform**, and **Python**, network operations can be treated as code, leading to more predictable, scalable, and efficient management.

1. **Key Principles of DevOps in Network Management**:
   - o **Collaboration**: DevOps encourages collaboration between development, IT operations, and network engineers to ensure that network configurations align with application requirements.
   - o **Automation**: DevOps aims to automate routine network tasks such as configuration management, software updates, monitoring, and performance analysis.
   - o **Continuous Integration and Delivery (CI/CD)**: CI/CD pipelines enable network configuration changes and updates to be tested, deployed, and rolled back efficiently and reliably.
   - o **Version Control**: Treating network configurations as code, storing them in version control systems like **Git**, helps maintain consistency and track changes over time.

2. **Challenges in Implementing DevOps for Network Management**:

- o **Complexity**: Network infrastructure can be complex, with multiple devices, protocols, and configurations that need to be managed.
- o **Integration**: Integrating network automation tools with existing DevOps tools and workflows can require careful planning and customization.
- o **Change Management**: Implementing changes in network infrastructure must be done with caution to avoid downtime or service disruption.

Using Python in CI/CD Pipelines for Network Automation

CI/CD pipelines are central to DevOps practices. These pipelines automate the process of integrating code changes, testing them, and deploying them to production. By leveraging Python in CI/CD pipelines, network automation tasks such as device configuration, monitoring, and provisioning can be automated and integrated into the software delivery lifecycle.

1. **Automating Network Configuration in CI/CD Pipelines**:

   Network configuration changes can be tested and deployed automatically through a CI/CD pipeline.

For example, Python scripts can be used to configure network devices (e.g., routers, switches) and ensure that configurations are applied consistently.

- o **Example: Integrating Python for Network Configuration Automation in a CI/CD Pipeline**:

  Here's how you can automate the application of network configurations as part of a CI/CD pipeline using **GitLab CI** (though it can be applied to other CI/CD tools like Jenkins, CircleCI, etc.):

  - **.gitlab-ci.yml (GitLab CI configuration file)**:

    ```yaml
    yaml

    stages:
      - test
      - deploy

    test_network_configuration:
      stage: test
      script:
    ```

```
-                python3
test_network_config.py  # Run
Python script to validate the
network configuration

deploy_network_configuration:
  stage: deploy
  script:
    -                python3
deploy_network_config.py    #
Deploy     the     validated
configuration using Python
  only:
    - master   # Run this job
only on the master branch
```

- **test_network_config.py (Test the Configuration)**:

```python

import subprocess

def test_ping(ip_address):
    try:
        response          =
subprocess.run(['ping', '-c',
'4',           ip_address],
stdout=subprocess.PIPE)
```

```
            if response.returncode
== 0:
            print(f"Ping      to
{ip_address} successful.")
        else:
            print(f"Ping      to
{ip_address} failed.")
            exit(1)
    except Exception as e:
        print(f"Error    pinging
{ip_address}: {e}")
        exit(1)


test_ping('192.168.1.1')      #
Example test for a router or
switch IP
```

- **deploy_network_config.py (Deploy the Configuration)**:

```python
python


from      netmiko      import
ConnectHandler

def
deploy_configuration(ip_addre
ss,    username,    password,
config_file):
    device = {
```

```
        'device_type':
'cisco_ios',
        'host': ip_address,
        'username': username,
        'password': password,
        'secret': password,
    }

    try:
        # Connect to the
device
        net_connect        =
ConnectHandler(**device)
        net_connect.enable()

        # Read configuration
file
        with open(config_file,
'r') as file:
            config_commands =
file.readlines()

        # Send configuration
to device

net_connect.send_config_set(c
onfig_commands)
        print(f"Configuration
applied to {ip_address}.")
```

269

```
         # Disconnect from the
device

net_connect.disconnect()

    except Exception as e:
        print(f"Error
deploying   configuration   to
{ip_address}: {e}")

deploy_configuration('192.168
.1.1',   'admin',   'password',
'network_config.txt')
```

o **Explanation**:

- The GitLab CI pipeline has two stages: **test** and **deploy**.
- The **test** stage uses Python to ping a network device and verify its availability.
- The **deploy** stage uses **Netmiko** to connect to a Cisco device and apply a configuration file, automating the process of applying configurations to network devices.
- By integrating these steps into a CI/CD pipeline, you ensure that network changes are tested and deployed

270

automatically, with minimal manual intervention.

2. **Automating Network Monitoring and Alerts in CI/CD Pipelines**:

CI/CD pipelines can also be used to monitor network performance and trigger alerts based on predefined thresholds. For instance, if a network device's latency exceeds a certain limit, an alert can be generated, and corrective actions can be taken.

- o **Example: Network Performance Monitoring in CI/CD**:
  - **`monitor_network_performance.py`**:

```python
python

import subprocess

def
monitor_latency(ip_address):
    result              =
subprocess.run(['ping', '-c',
'4',              ip_address],
stdout=subprocess.PIPE)
    output              =
result.stdout.decode('utf-8')
```

271

```
# Extract average latency
avg_latency          =
float(output.split('=')[-
1].split('/')[1])


    if avg_latency > 100:  #
Latency threshold of 100 ms
        print(f"Warning:  High
latency        detected      -
{avg_latency} ms.")
        return False
    else:
        print(f"Latency      to
{ip_address}:    {avg_latency}
ms.")
        return True


if                        not
monitor_latency('192.168.1.1'
):
    exit(1)     #  Fail   the
pipeline  if  latency  exceeds
threshold
```

- **Explanation**:
  - This Python script runs a **ping** test to monitor the network latency to a specific IP address.

272

If the latency exceeds a predefined threshold (e.g., 100 ms), it will fail the pipeline and trigger an alert or further action.

Automating Network Infrastructure as Code

Infrastructure as Code (IaC) is a key practice in DevOps, allowing network configurations and resources to be defined and managed using code. Python, together with IaC tools like **Terraform**, **Ansible**, or **CloudFormation**, can automate the entire process of provisioning and managing network infrastructure.

1. **Using Python to Automate Infrastructure as Code with Terraform**:

   Terraform is a popular IaC tool that allows you to define cloud infrastructure using configuration files (written in HCL—HashiCorp Configuration Language). Python can be used to automate the execution of **Terraform** commands in CI/CD pipelines or as standalone tools for provisioning network resources.

273

o **Example: Automating Terraform Commands with Python**:

```python
python

import subprocess

def run_terraform_command(command):
    try:
        result = subprocess.run(['terraform', command], stdout=subprocess.PIPE, stderr=subprocess.PIPE)
        if result.returncode == 0:
            print(result.stdout.decode('utf-8'))
        else:
            print(f"Error running terraform command: {result.stderr.decode('utf-8')}")
    except Exception as e:
        print(f"Error executing Terraform command: {e}")

# Initialize Terraform and apply configuration
run_terraform_command('init')
```

274

```
run_terraform_command('apply -auto-
approve')
```

- o **Explanation**:
  - The Python script runs **Terraform** commands such as `terraform init` (to initialize the configuration) and `terraform apply` (to apply the infrastructure defined in the Terraform configuration files).
  - Automating these steps in Python allows you to integrate **Terraform** into your CI/CD pipeline for dynamic provisioning of network resources.

2. **Using Python and Ansible for Network Automation as Code**:

Ansible can be used to automate network tasks like configuration management and provisioning, while Python can trigger Ansible playbooks and handle configuration files programmatically.

- o **Example: Automating Network Configuration with Ansible and Python**:

```
python
```

275

```
import subprocess

def
run_ansible_playbook(playbook_path)
:
    try:
        subprocess.run(['ansible-
playbook',           playbook_path],
check=True)
        print(f"Successfully applied
Ansible playbook: {playbook_path}")
    except
subprocess.CalledProcessError as e:
        print(f"Error        running
playbook: {e}")

# Example usage
run_ansible_playbook('network_confi
g.yml')
```

- o **Explanation**:
    - The Python script runs an **Ansible playbook** that automates network configurations using Python as a controller.
    - This approach treats network configurations as code, ensuring that

276

network devices are consistently configured according to the playbook.

Conclusion

In this chapter, we've explored how **DevOps** practices can be applied to **network management** through automation, focusing on how Python integrates with **CI/CD pipelines** and **Infrastructure as Code** (IaC) tools like **Terraform** and **Ansible**. By automating network tasks such as configuration management, network monitoring, and infrastructure provisioning, network administrators can achieve more efficient, scalable, and reliable network operations. The use of Python in network automation enables consistent network configurations, rapid deployment of resources, and proactive network performance optimization, ultimately driving improvements in the network's overall health and stability.

CHAPTER 22

TESTING NETWORK AUTOMATION SCRIPTS

Best Practices for Testing Network Automation Scripts

Testing network automation scripts is crucial to ensure that they work as expected and that they do not cause disruptions to network infrastructure. Given the critical nature of network configurations and automation, testing helps detect issues early, improve reliability, and maintain consistency. Below are some best practices for testing network automation scripts effectively.

1. **Define Clear Testing Objectives**:
   - o Identify the primary goal of your automation script (e.g., backup configurations, configure QoS, monitor performance).
   - o Define expected outcomes before testing the script, such as ensuring a configuration change is applied, network devices are reachable, or a task is completed without errors.
2. **Test in a Controlled Environment**:

- o Always test network automation scripts in a **lab** or **staging environment** before applying them to production. This helps ensure that the scripts don't inadvertently disrupt live systems.
- o Use **virtualized environments** such as **GNS3** or **Cisco Packet Tracer** to create test networks that mimic real-world scenarios.

3. **Version Control for Network Scripts**:

- o Store network automation scripts in a version control system (e.g., **Git**) to track changes, roll back to previous versions, and ensure consistency across environments.
- o Use **Git hooks** to trigger tests automatically when changes are made to the scripts.

4. **Ensure Idempotency**:

- o Idempotency ensures that scripts can be run multiple times without causing unintended side effects or errors.
- o For example, running a configuration backup script multiple times should not overwrite or cause conflicts with the backup files.

5. **Monitor Logs and Outputs**:

- o Always capture logs and outputs during script execution to review and debug. Logs can provide important insights into why a task failed or succeeded.

o   Implement logging within your scripts to track actions, exceptions, and status updates.

6. **Create Comprehensive Test Cases**:

o   Include tests for edge cases, such as unexpected network states (e.g., device down, invalid configurations) and error handling.

o   Ensure that your test cases include scenarios for success and failure.

Unit Testing and Integration Testing for Network Automation

1. **Unit Testing**: Unit testing focuses on testing individual components or functions of the automation script to ensure that each part works in isolation. Python provides several testing frameworks for unit testing, such as **unittest** and **pytest**.

   o   **Example: Unit Test for Network Automation Script**: Suppose we have a Python function that pings a network device to verify its reachability:

```python
python
```

```python
def ping_device(ip_address):
```

280

```
import subprocess
result = subprocess.run(['ping',
'-c',      '4',      ip_address],
stdout=subprocess.PIPE,
stderr=subprocess.PIPE)
    if result.returncode == 0:
        return True
    else:
        return False
```

We can write a unit test to verify that this function behaves as expected:

```
python
```

```
import unittest
from unittest.mock import patch
from your_script import ping_device

class
TestPingDevice(unittest.TestCase):

    @patch('subprocess.run')
    def    test_ping_success(self,
mock_run):
        # Mock the subprocess.run
method to simulate a successful ping

mock_run.return_value.returncode = 0
```

281

```
        result                      =
ping_device('192.168.1.1')
        self.assertTrue(result)


    @patch('subprocess.run')
    def      test_ping_failure(self,
mock_run):
        # Mock the subprocess.run
method to simulate a failed ping

mock_run.return_value.returncode = 1
        result                      =
ping_device('192.168.1.1')
        self.assertFalse(result)


if __name__ == '__main__':
    unittest.main()
```

o **Explanation**:

- **unittest** is used to define the test case
  for the ping_device function.
- The patch decorator is used to mock the
  subprocess.run method to simulate
  both successful and failed pings, without
  actually sending network requests.
- This test ensures that the ping_device
  function correctly returns True or False
  based on the ping result.

282

2. **Integration Testing**: Integration testing ensures that different components or services in the network automation script work together as expected. For network automation, integration tests typically involve running scripts that interact with real or simulated network devices, verifying that changes are applied, and ensuring connectivity.

   o **Example: Integration Test for Network Automation**: Consider an integration test for a script that backs up a network device's configuration using **Netmiko**:

```python
from netmiko import ConnectHandler

def
backup_device_configuration(ip_addr
ess, username, password):
    device = {
        'device_type': 'cisco_ios',
        'host': ip_address,
        'username': username,
        'password': password,
    }
    try:
```

```
        net_connect         =
ConnectHandler(**device)
        config              =
net_connect.send_command('show
running-config')
        return config
    except Exception as e:
        return str(e)


def
test_backup_device_configuration():
    # Test with a real or virtual
device IP address
    config                  =
backup_device_configuration('192.16
8.1.1', 'admin', 'password')
    assert isinstance(config, str)
and 'interface' in config  # Ensure
the backup contains the expected data
```

- o **Explanation**:
    - In this example, the function `backup_device_configuration` uses **Netmiko** to connect to a Cisco device and retrieve its running configuration.
    - The test checks that the backup contains the expected configuration data by asserting that the returned configuration

284

is a string containing the word `interface`.

Tools and Libraries for Network Automation Testing

1. **unittest (Unit Testing)**:
   - **unittest** is the built-in Python testing framework and follows the xUnit style. It allows for defining test cases, asserting conditions, and running tests in a structured manner. It's ideal for unit testing smaller functions or components in a network automation script.
   - **Features**:
     - Built-in assertion methods (e.g., `assertEqual`, `assertTrue`).
     - Supports test discovery and running tests in suites.
     - Supports setup and teardown methods for preparing and cleaning up test environments.
   - **Example**: Running all tests in a script:

   ```bash
   bash
   ```

285

```
python          -m          unittest
test_your_script.py
```

2. pytest (Unit and Integration Testing):

- o **pytest** is a more flexible and powerful testing framework compared to `unittest`. It supports advanced features such as fixtures, parameterized tests, and detailed reporting.

- o **Features**:
  - Simple syntax for writing test functions.
  - Powerful assertions (e.g., `assert expr1 == expr2`).
  - Support for plugins and integrations.
  - Automatic test discovery and execution.

- o **Example**:

```python
python

import pytest
from your_script import ping_device

def test_ping_success():
    assert
ping_device('192.168.1.1') == True

def test_ping_failure():
```

286

```
assert
ping_device('192.168.1.100')    ==
False
```

- To run the tests:

```
bash
```

```
pytest test_your_script.py
```

3. **Mocking and Patching (unittest.mock or pytest-mock)**:

   o **Mocking** and **patching** are essential for testing network automation scripts that interact with external systems, such as network devices. The **unittest.mock** module or the **pytest-mock** plugin helps simulate external calls and test network automation scripts in isolation.

   o **Example** (using **pytest-mock**):

```python
def test_ping_device(mocker):
    mock_ping          =
mocker.patch('subprocess.run')

mock_ping.return_value.returncode    =
0
```

287

```
assert
ping_device('192.168.1.1') == True
```

4. Test Automation Frameworks:

o **Robot Framework** is an open-source automation framework for acceptance testing and robotic process automation (RPA). It's great for network automation testing when combined with libraries like **SSHLibrary** and **Netmiko.**

o **Example** (simple test case in Robot Framework):

```
robot

*** Settings ***
Library     SSHLibrary

*** Variables ***
${HOST}     192.168.1.1
${USER}     admin
${PASS}     password

*** Test Cases ***
Test Ping Device
    Open   Connection          ${HOST}
${USER}     ${PASS}
    ${result}=      Execute   Command
ping -c 4 ${HOST}
    Should Contain    ${result}    0%
packet loss
```

288

Conclusion

In this chapter, we've discussed best practices for testing network automation scripts, the importance of unit and integration testing, and the tools available for effective testing. Testing network automation scripts ensures that your scripts work as expected, are reliable, and can be safely deployed in production environments. By using Python's powerful testing frameworks, such as **unittest**, **pytest**, and mocking libraries, network administrators can ensure that their automation solutions remain robust, stable, and effective over time. Testing is an integral part of the development process, enabling faster, safer, and more reliable network automation at scale.

CHAPTER 23

TROUBLESHOOTING PYTHON NETWORK AUTOMATION SCRIPTS

Common Issues and Pitfalls in Network Automation with Python

Network automation with Python provides great flexibility, but it also comes with its own set of challenges. Below are some of the most common issues and pitfalls that network automation engineers face when using Python for automating network tasks.

1. **Connection Failures (SSH, Telnet, SNMP)**:
   o **Issue**: A common problem in network automation scripts is failing to connect to network devices using protocols such as SSH, Telnet, or SNMP.
   o **Common Causes**:
     ▪ Incorrect credentials (username, password, or enable password).
     ▪ SSH or Telnet not enabled or misconfigured on the device.

290

- Network issues such as firewall rules blocking the connection or unreachable IP addresses.
- Mismatched or unsupported SSH versions between the Python client and the network device.

o **Solution**:

- Double-check credentials and ensure the SSH service is running on the target device.
- Use **Netmiko**'s error handling to catch exceptions when establishing connections.
- Use **ping** tests or **traceroute** to ensure network connectivity.

2. **Timeouts and Latency Issues**:

o **Issue**: Scripts can often experience timeouts or delays due to high network latency or devices taking longer to respond than expected.

o **Common Causes**:

- Devices are under heavy load or misconfigured, causing slow responses.
- Long command outputs or waiting for the device to process configurations.

o **Solution**:

- Increase the timeout settings in libraries like **Netmiko** (via the `timeout` parameter).
- Use Python's **subprocess** library to monitor execution times and handle timeouts gracefully with **try-except** blocks.

3. **Incorrect or Missing Configurations**:
   - **Issue**: Automation scripts that modify network configurations (e.g., applying VLANs, interfaces, routing protocols) may fail due to incorrect or incomplete configurations.
   - **Common Causes**:
     - Missing parameters in configuration commands.
     - Configurations that are not compatible with the device's current state.
     - Configuration drift where changes in one part of the network affect other parts.
   - **Solution**:
     - Before applying changes, always verify the current device configuration using commands like `show running-config`.

292

- Test configuration changes in a controlled environment to ensure compatibility before applying them in production.
- Use **Netmiko** or **Ansible** to perform dry-runs or "test" configurations on devices.

4. **Inconsistent or Unreliable Network State**:
   - **Issue**: In large or dynamic networks, the state of devices can change frequently, causing automation scripts to behave unpredictably.
   - **Common Causes**:
     - Fluctuating network conditions (e.g., device reboots, link failures, IP address changes).
     - Devices being offline or out of sync with automation scripts due to manual changes or outages.
   - **Solution**:
     - Implement robust **error handling** in your scripts to detect and recover from failures.
     - Consider integrating network state verification steps within your automation scripts to ensure devices are in the expected state before performing tasks.

5. **Inadequate Logging and Error Handling**:

o **Issue**: Many automation scripts lack adequate logging or error handling, making it difficult to diagnose issues when things go wrong.

o **Common Causes**:

- Lack of proper log messages or excessive silent failures.

- Incomplete exception handling, leading to script crashes or incorrect behavior.

o **Solution**:

- Use Python's built-in **logging** module to capture log messages at different levels (e.g., INFO, WARNING, ERROR) to track script execution and issues.

- Implement comprehensive **try-except** blocks to handle known exceptions (e.g., timeouts, connection errors) and log errors for debugging.

Debugging and Optimizing Scripts for Efficiency

When automation scripts are not behaving as expected, debugging and optimization are necessary to improve their reliability and efficiency.

1. **Debugging Network Automation Scripts**:

Debugging helps identify issues in the script's logic, connectivity, and flow. Python provides several tools and techniques to help with this process.

- o **Use Print Statements or Logging**:
  - Add print statements or logging at key points in your script to output values of variables and identify where it fails.
  - Python's **logging** module allows you to control the level of detail in your logs (e.g., DEBUG, INFO, ERROR).
  - Example:

```python

import logging
logging.basicConfig(level=log
ging.DEBUG)

def connect_to_device(ip):

logging.debug(f"Attempting to
connect to {ip}")
    # Your connection logic
here
```

- o **Use Python's Debugger (pdb)**:

- The **pdb** module allows you to step through the script, inspect variables, and evaluate expressions at runtime.

- Example:

```python
python
```

```python
import pdb
```

```python
def test_function():
    x = 10
    pdb.set_trace()    # Start
debugging here
    y = 20
    result = x + y
    print(result)
```

```python
test_function()
```

- Use `pdb` commands like `n` (next), `c` (continue), `q` (quit) to step through the code.

o **Simulate Network Conditions**:

- To troubleshoot network-related issues, you can use tools like **ping**, **traceroute**, or network simulation tools (e.g., **GNS3** or **Cisco Packet Tracer**) to simulate

296

network latency, packet loss, and link failure.

2. **Optimizing Network Automation Scripts**:

After debugging, it's essential to optimize the script for performance, reliability, and scalability.

- **Limit the Number of API Calls**:
  - Minimize the number of requests made to network devices or APIs, as excessive requests can slow down the script or lead to rate-limiting.
  - Batch commands or use **bulk configuration commands** when interacting with devices.
- **Efficiently Handle Large Command Outputs**:
  - For devices that produce large outputs (e.g., `show running-config`), consider filtering the output or capturing only the relevant information to reduce overhead.
  - Use Python's **subprocess** module to capture command output efficiently and process it in chunks.
- **Leverage Parallel Execution**:

- Use Python's **concurrent.futures** or **asyncio** to run multiple tasks in parallel when managing multiple devices. This can speed up tasks such as device configuration or monitoring.

- Example using `concurrent.futures`:

```python
from concurrent.futures import ThreadPoolExecutor

def configure_device(device_ip):
    # Configure the device
    pass

with ThreadPoolExecutor(max_workers=10) as executor:

executor.map(configure_device, ['192.168.1.1', '192.168.1.2', '192.168.1.3'])
```

  o **Cache Results**:

- If a script repeatedly fetches the same data (e.g., device configurations or performance stats), consider caching the

298

results temporarily to avoid redundant API calls.

Best Practices for Maintaining Python Automation Scripts

Maintaining Python automation scripts ensures they remain reliable, scalable, and adaptable to changing network environments.

1. **Use Version Control (Git)**:
   o Store your scripts in a **Git** repository to track changes, collaborate with others, and roll back to previous versions when necessary.
   o Use branches for different features and maintain a main branch for stable versions.

2. **Modularize and Reuse Code**:
   o Break your scripts into modular, reusable functions or classes. This makes it easier to maintain and update scripts as the network environment evolves.
   o For example, separate functions for connecting to devices, applying configurations, and monitoring performance.

3. **Write Clear and Maintainable Code**:

- o Use meaningful variable and function names, write docstrings for functions and classes, and add comments explaining complex logic.
- o Example:

```python

def    get_device_status(ip_address,
timeout=10):
    """
    Retrieves the current status of
the network device.

    :param   ip_address:   The    IP
address of the device to check
    :param timeout: Time to wait for
a response from the device
    :return: Status of the device
    """
    # Code to get status
    pass
```

4. Document and Version Automation Scripts:

- o Keep a **readme** file in your repository to document how to use the scripts, dependencies, and the network environment they are designed for.

o Include a **changelog** to track updates, bug fixes, and new features.

5. **Automate Testing**:

o Use continuous integration tools (e.g., **GitLab CI**, **Jenkins**) to automatically test network automation scripts whenever changes are made.

o This helps catch issues early and ensures that new changes do not break existing functionality.

6. **Monitor Script Performance**:

o Keep track of how well your scripts perform in real-world scenarios. Use logging to monitor execution time and identify bottlenecks.

7. **Handle Failures Gracefully**:

o Add **error handling** to ensure that your script can handle issues like network device unavailability, timeouts, and incorrect configurations without causing disruption.

o For example, use **try-except** blocks to handle connection failures or device unavailability:

python

```
try:
    # Connection code
except Exception as e:
    logging.error(f"Connection    to
device failed: {e}")
```

8. **Regularly Review and Refactor Code**:
   o Network infrastructure and devices evolve over time, and so should your scripts. Regularly review and refactor your scripts to incorporate new features or improve performance.
   o Ensure that your scripts are compatible with the latest network device models and OS versions.

Conclusion

In this chapter, we've explored common issues and pitfalls encountered when automating network tasks with Python, as well as techniques for debugging and optimizing network automation scripts. Effective troubleshooting and optimization help ensure that your automation scripts are efficient, reliable, and scalable. By following best practices for maintaining Python scripts, such as using version control, modularizing code, and automating tests, you can ensure that your network automation efforts continue to drive efficiency and consistency in network management.

CHAPTER 24

SCALING NETWORK AUTOMATION

Scaling Network Automation Scripts for Large Networks

As network infrastructures grow, automating large-scale configurations, monitoring, and management tasks becomes essential to maintain efficiency and reduce the risk of human error. Python, with its extensive libraries and tools, offers the flexibility to scale network automation scripts effectively for large networks, handling a vast number of devices and configurations.

1. **Challenges of Scaling Network Automation**:
   - **Device Heterogeneity**: Large networks often include a wide range of devices from different vendors with varying configurations and APIs.
   - **Network Latency**: As the number of devices increases, network latency and timeouts become a concern, especially when managing devices in remote or geographically distributed locations.

o **Configuration Drift**: Over time, manual changes or inconsistent configurations can lead to configuration drift, where devices across the network no longer align with the desired configuration baseline.

o **Error Handling**: Handling errors at scale becomes more complex, especially when devices may be offline, configurations fail to apply, or network conditions fluctuate.

2. **Techniques for Scaling Network Automation Scripts**:

o **Parallel Execution**: Running tasks on multiple devices concurrently can drastically reduce the time it takes to complete automation tasks across a large network.

o **Task Queuing and Scheduling**: Use job queues (e.g., **Celery**, **RabbitMQ**) to schedule and distribute tasks across multiple workers for large-scale operations like device configuration or monitoring.

o **Asynchronous Execution**: Python's **asyncio** allows asynchronous I/O, enabling non-blocking operations for tasks like device configuration, monitoring, and data collection.

- o **Batch Processing**: When dealing with a large number of devices, batch processing can help manage devices in groups, applying configurations or running tests in phases to reduce load.

- o **Example: Running Tasks in Parallel with ThreadPoolExecutor**:

```python
from concurrent.futures import ThreadPoolExecutor
import time

def configure_device(device_ip):
    print(f"Configuring {device_ip}")
    # Simulate a network operation
    time.sleep(2)
    print(f"Device {device_ip} configured.")

device_ips = ['192.168.1.1', '192.168.1.2', '192.168.1.3']

with ThreadPoolExecutor(max_workers=5) as executor:
```

```
executor.map(configure_device,
device_ips)
```

- o **Explanation**:
  - This example uses `ThreadPoolExecutor` to configure multiple devices in parallel, improving the speed of the task when managing a large number of devices.

Using Python for Large-Scale Configuration Management and Monitoring

1. **Configuration Management at Scale**: For large networks, automating the configuration of devices becomes a challenge due to the sheer number of devices and the diversity of configurations required. **Ansible**, **SaltStack**, and **Terraform** are commonly used in conjunction with Python to manage configurations at scale. These tools can be integrated with Python to apply consistent configurations across thousands of devices.

   - o **Example: Using Ansible for Configuration Management**: Ansible playbooks can be controlled from Python to deploy

306

configurations across large numbers of devices. Here's an example using Python to run an Ansible playbook:

```python
import subprocess

def run_ansible_playbook(playbook_path):
    subprocess.run(['ansible-playbook', playbook_path], check=True)
    print(f"Playbook {playbook_path} executed successfully.")

# Example usage
run_ansible_playbook('configure_network.yml')
```

- o **Explanation**:
  - ▪ This Python script calls an **Ansible playbook**, which applies configurations to a large group of network devices. Ansible handles the distribution of tasks, while Python orchestrates the execution.

307

2. **Monitoring Network Devices at Scale**: Monitoring thousands of devices for performance, availability, and security requires efficient automation. Python can be used to collect metrics such as bandwidth utilization, latency, and uptime from devices, store this data, and generate alerts when thresholds are exceeded.

- o **Example: Using SNMP for Large-Scale Monitoring**: Here's an example of using Python and **PySNMP** to monitor devices across a large network:

```python
from pysnmp.hlapi import *
from concurrent.futures import ThreadPoolExecutor

def get_device_uptime(ip):
    iterator = getCmd(SnmpEngine(),

CommunityData('public'),

UdpTransportTarget((ip, 161)),

ContextData(),
```

```python
ObjectType(ObjectIdentity('1.3.6.1.
2.1.1.3.0')))

    error_indication, error_status,
error_index,        var_binds       =
next(iterator)

    if error_indication:
        print(f"Error:
{error_indication}")
    else:
        uptime = var_binds[0][1]
        print(f"Device {ip} uptime:
{uptime}")
        return uptime

def monitor_devices(device_ips):
    with ThreadPoolExecutor() as
executor:
        return
list(executor.map(get_device_uptime
, device_ips))

# Example usage
device_ips    =    ['192.168.1.1',
'192.168.1.2', '192.168.1.3']
monitor_devices(device_ips)
```

o **Explanation**:

- This script uses **PySNMP** to query the uptime of multiple devices concurrently, leveraging `ThreadPoolExecutor` to run the queries in parallel. This allows the monitoring of a large network with minimal delay.

Managing Multiple Devices with Scalable Automation Frameworks

To manage thousands of devices, it is important to use scalable frameworks that can automate the deployment and management of network configurations, monitoring, and maintenance tasks.

1. **Ansible**:

   o **Ansible** is a powerful automation tool that can be used in large-scale environments. It uses **playbooks** written in **YAML**, which describe the tasks to be performed on devices. Python can control Ansible and automate the execution of playbooks, especially when dealing with hundreds or thousands of devices.

   o **Features**:

- **Agentless**: No need to install agents on network devices.
- **Idempotent**: Ensures that tasks are applied only when necessary.
- **Scalability**: Ansible can manage thousands of devices by distributing tasks across multiple machines.

o **Example: Automating Network Configuration with Ansible**:

```python
python

import subprocess

def run_ansible_playbook(playbook_path, inventory_path):
    subprocess.run(['ansible-playbook', '-i', inventory_path, playbook_path], check=True)
    print(f"Successfully ran playbook: {playbook_path}")

# Example usage
run_ansible_playbook('configure_network.yml', 'inventory.ini')
```

2. **SaltStack**:

311

- o **SaltStack** is another automation tool designed for scalability. It is especially useful for managing a large number of devices across geographically dispersed locations.

- o **Features**:
  - **Push and Pull Models**: Can push configuration changes or pull information from devices.
  - **Real-time Execution**: Provides fast communication between master and minion nodes for real-time task execution.
  - **Scalable**: Suitable for large networks due to its efficient communication model.

- o **Example: Managing Devices with SaltStack**:
  - The **Salt client** can be controlled through Python, allowing you to execute tasks across thousands of devices concurrently.

```python

import salt.client

def execute_salt_command(command):
```

```
    client                      =
salt.client.LocalClient()
    result    =    client.cmd('*',
'cmd.run', [command])
    return result


# Example usage
result = execute_salt_command('show
version')
print(result)
```

3. **Terraform**:

   o **Terraform** is widely used for managing cloud infrastructure, but it can also be leveraged for managing network devices and configurations. Using **Python** to interact with **Terraform** allows you to automate network provisioning and scaling by managing network resources as code.

   o **Example: Terraform Automation with Python**:

```python
python


import subprocess


def run_terraform_apply():
```

313

```
    subprocess.run(['terraform',
'apply',              '-auto-approve'],
check=True)
    print("Terraform apply executed
successfully.")


run_terraform_apply()
```

- o **Explanation**:
  - This Python script triggers the execution of **Terraform** to provision or modify network resources as defined in Terraform files.
  - Terraform ensures that configurations are applied consistently across multiple devices and cloud resources.

Conclusion

In this chapter, we explored how to scale network automation scripts for large networks, focusing on efficient management, monitoring, and configuration tasks. By leveraging Python in conjunction with scalable frameworks like **Ansible**, **SaltStack**, and **Terraform**, network engineers can automate large-scale network operations, reducing manual errors and improving efficiency. Additionally, by utilizing techniques like parallel execution, task scheduling, and asynchronous execution, Python can be optimized to handle large networks seamlessly. Ultimately, scaling network automation allows organizations to manage complex and geographically dispersed networks more effectively, ensuring consistency, speed, and reliability across the infrastructure.

CHAPTER 25

INTEGRATING PYTHON WITH NETWORK ANALYTICS TOOLS

Automating Network Analytics Tasks

Network analytics tools are crucial for monitoring network performance, detecting issues, and optimizing network traffic. Automating network analytics tasks with Python can significantly reduce manual intervention, allowing for real-time insights, predictive analysis, and rapid troubleshooting. Python's flexibility and ability to integrate with various network analytics platforms make it an ideal tool for automating and enhancing network monitoring.

1. **Automation of Data Collection and Reporting**:
   o   Many network analytics tools collect and store vast amounts of performance data (e.g., bandwidth usage, latency, packet loss, etc.). Python can automate the extraction, processing, and reporting of this data to provide meaningful insights.

o Python scripts can be scheduled to pull data from analytics platforms periodically, generate reports, and send them to network administrators or trigger alerts when certain thresholds are exceeded.

2. **Automating Alert Management**:

o Network monitoring tools often generate alerts for events like high traffic, device failure, or security breaches. Python can automate the management of these alerts by processing them and triggering corrective actions such as restarting services or rerouting traffic.

o Python can also integrate with communication platforms (e.g., email, Slack, or SMS) to notify network administrators in real-time about critical events.

3. **Integration with APIs for Automation**:

o Many network analytics platforms expose APIs that allow for the automation of tasks such as data retrieval, configuration, and event management. Python can interact with these APIs to automate workflows, integrate multiple tools, or consolidate data from various sources.

o By using Python's **requests** library or platform-specific SDKs, network automation tasks such as

317

fetching performance metrics, configuring devices, or managing alerts can be automated.

Using Python to Process Data from Network Analytics Platforms

Network analytics platforms like **SolarWinds**, **Nagios**, **PRTG**, and **Zabbix** provide comprehensive monitoring capabilities for managing network performance. Python can be used to process the data generated by these platforms, automate actions based on predefined criteria, and integrate with other systems for enhanced visibility and response.

1. **SolarWinds Integration**:
    o **SolarWinds** provides powerful network monitoring tools with a comprehensive API that allows you to query device data, performance metrics, and configurations.
    o **Python Integration**: You can use Python to interact with the SolarWinds API to fetch performance data, automate reporting, or trigger alerts.
    o **Example: Fetching Performance Data from SolarWinds API**: SolarWinds offers a

REST API that you can interact with using Python's `requests` library.

```python
import requests
from requests.auth import HTTPBasicAuth
import json

def get_solarwinds_data(api_url, username, password):
    # API endpoint to fetch network performance data
    endpoint = f"{api_url}/Swis/Rest/V3/Nodes"

    # Basic authentication for SolarWinds API
    auth = HTTPBasicAuth(username, password)

    # Send GET request to fetch data
    response = requests.get(endpoint, auth=auth)

    if response.status_code == 200:
        # Process the JSON data
        data = response.json()
```

319

```
        return data
    else:
        print(f"Failed    to    fetch
data: {response.status_code}")
        return None

# Example usage
api_url                              =
"https://your_solarwinds_server"
username = "admin"
password = "password"
nodes = get_solarwinds_data(api_url,
username, password)
if nodes:
    print(json.dumps(nodes,
indent=4))
```

- o **Explanation**:
  - The script uses **SolarWinds API** to fetch data related to network nodes (e.g., device status, performance metrics).
  - The response is processed as **JSON** and displayed in a human-readable format.
  - This can be expanded to generate reports, check device status, or integrate with other systems for automated responses.

2. **Nagios Integration**:

- o **Nagios** is a popular open-source monitoring system that allows monitoring of network services, host resources, and servers. It also provides an API for querying performance data, managing services, and handling events.

- o **Example: Retrieving Nagios Alerts and Performance Data**: Nagios can be queried using its **JSON API** to retrieve performance metrics and active alerts.

```python
import requests

def get_nagios_data(nagios_api_url,
username, password):
    # API endpoint for Nagios
performance data
    endpoint                =
f"{nagios_api_url}/objects/hoststat
us"

    # Send GET request with
authentication
```

```
    response                    =
requests.get(endpoint,
auth=(username, password))

    if response.status_code == 200:
        data = response.json()
        return data
    else:
        print(f"Failed    to    fetch
Nagios                        data:
{response.status_code}")
        return None

# Example usage
nagios_api_url                 =
"http://nagios_server/nagiosxi/api/
v1"
username = "admin"
password = "password"
host_status                    =
get_nagios_data(nagios_api_url,
username, password)
if host_status:
    print(host_status)
```

- o **Explanation**:
  - ▪ The script fetches the **host status** data from Nagios using the **JSON API**.

- This allows Python to automatically retrieve network monitoring data and integrate it with other systems or trigger actions based on alerts.

3. **PRTG Network Monitoring Integration**:

   o **PRTG** provides robust monitoring capabilities and has an open API for managing devices, sensors, and performance metrics.

   o Python can interact with the PRTG API to retrieve data, configure sensors, and automate the monitoring of network performance.

   o **Example: Accessing PRTG Data Using Python**:

```python
import requests

def         get_prtg_data(prtg_url,
api_key):
    # Endpoint to fetch sensors from
PRTG
    endpoint                    =
f"{prtg_url}/api/table.json?content
=sensors&output=json&columns=device
```

323

```
,group,priority,status&api_key={api
_key}"

    # Send GET request to fetch data
    response                         =
requests.get(endpoint)

    if response.status_code == 200:
        data = response.json()
        return data
    else:
        print(f"Failed to fetch PRTG
data: {response.status_code}")
        return None

# Example usage
prtg_url                             =
"https://your_prtg_server"
api_key = "your_api_key"
sensors   =   get_prtg_data(prtg_url,
api_key)
if sensors:
    print(sensors)
```

o **Explanation**:

- The script fetches **sensor data** from
  PRTG, which includes device status,
  priority, and monitoring metrics.

- This can be extended to automate the management of sensors, configuration of alerts, or reporting on network performance.

Real-World Example of Integrating Python Scripts with Network Monitoring Systems

In a real-world scenario, Python can be integrated with a network monitoring system to automate the collection of data, analyze network performance, and trigger actions based on predefined thresholds. Here is an example that integrates data collection from multiple network monitoring systems, processes it, and triggers an action based on certain conditions.

Example: Automating Network Health Checks with Python

This script integrates with **Nagios**, **PRTG**, and **SolarWinds** to retrieve network device health data and take action if certain performance metrics are exceeded.

```python
python

import requests
```

```python
import smtplib
from email.mime.text import MIMEText

# Fetch Nagios, PRTG, and SolarWinds data
def get_nagios_data():
    # Replace with your Nagios API details
    endpoint                              =
"http://nagios_server/api/v1/objects/hoststatus
"
    response        =        requests.get(endpoint,
auth=('admin', 'password'))
    return response.json()


def get_prtg_data():
    # Replace with your PRTG API details
    endpoint                              =
"https://prtg_server/api/table.json?content=sen
sors&output=json&api_key=your_api_key"
    response = requests.get(endpoint)
    return response.json()


def get_solarwinds_data():
    # Replace with your SolarWinds API details
    endpoint                              =
"https://solarwinds_server/Swis/Rest/V3/Nodes"
    response        =        requests.get(endpoint,
auth=('admin', 'password'))
    return response.json()
```

```python
# Check if any device exceeds thresholds
def check_device_status():
    nagios_data = get_nagios_data()
    prtg_data = get_prtg_data()
    solarwinds_data = get_solarwinds_data()

    # Example condition: if any device status is
'down' or latency exceeds threshold
    for device in nagios_data['hoststatus']:
        if device['status'] == 'down':
            send_alert(f"Device {device['name']}
is down (Nagios).")

    for sensor in prtg_data['sensors']:
        if sensor['status'] == 'down':
            send_alert(f"Sensor
{sensor['device']} is down (PRTG).")

    for node in solarwinds_data['nodes']:
        if node['status'] != 'Up':
            send_alert(f"Node {node['name']} is
not up (SolarWinds).")

# Send an email alert
def send_alert(message):
    msg = MIMEText(message)
    msg['Subject'] = 'Network Alert: Performance
Issue Detected'
    msg['From'] = 'your_email@example.com'
```

```
msg['To'] = 'admin@example.com'

with   smtplib.SMTP('smtp.example.com')   as
server:
    server.sendmail(msg['From'],
[msg['To']], msg.as_string())
    print(f"Alert sent: {message}")


# Run the network health check
check_device_status()
```

Explanation:

- This script integrates data from **Nagios**, **PRTG**, and **SolarWinds** to fetch the health status of devices across the network.
- If any device or sensor is down or exceeds certain thresholds (e.g., high latency), an email alert is sent to the administrator.
- Python's flexibility allows seamless integration between different monitoring platforms, making it easy to aggregate data and trigger automated actions.

Conclusion

In this chapter, we've explored how Python can be used to automate network analytics tasks, process data from network monitoring platforms like **SolarWinds**, **Nagios**, and **PRTG**, and integrate with these systems to enhance network monitoring and management. Python's ability to interact with APIs, process performance metrics, and automate tasks ensures that network administrators can gain real-time insights, respond proactively to issues, and maintain optimal network performance. The real-world example demonstrated how Python scripts can integrate data from multiple sources, analyze it, and take actions automatically, ultimately improving network efficiency and reducing manual intervention.

CHAPTER 26

SECURITY BEST PRACTICES FOR NETWORK AUTOMATION

Security Considerations When Automating Network Management Tasks

Network automation involves a wide array of tasks, from configuring devices and monitoring network performance to managing security policies and integrating with external systems. While automation brings significant benefits, it also introduces security risks. These risks need to be managed carefully to ensure that automation does not become a vector for attacks, breaches, or unauthorized access. Below are key security considerations when automating network management tasks.

1. **Minimize Attack Surface**:
    o   Automation scripts often interact with multiple network devices and systems, which increases the potential attack surface. It's crucial to minimize exposure by:

- Limiting the number of devices or systems the scripts can interact with.
- Restricting access to automation systems using firewalls, VPNs, or secure tunnels.
- Using **read-only** access when possible, especially for monitoring tasks, to minimize the potential impact of unauthorized changes.

2. **Use Encryption**:

   o Sensitive data such as **device credentials**, **configuration files**, and **API tokens** must be encrypted both in transit and at rest. Always use secure protocols such as **SSH, HTTPS**, and **SFTP** for communication between automation scripts and network devices.

   o **TLS/SSL** should be used for encrypting data transmitted over networks, particularly when APIs are involved.

   o Store sensitive information such as passwords and keys in **encrypted vaults** (e.g., **HashiCorp Vault, AWS Secrets Manager, Azure Key Vault**) instead of hardcoding them in the scripts.

3. **Logging and Monitoring**:

   o Automated scripts must generate detailed logs of all activities, including configuration changes, device interactions, and errors. This helps detect suspicious activities and enables forensics in case of security incidents.

o Ensure logs are stored securely and are regularly monitored for unusual behavior, such as unauthorized access attempts or unexpected configuration changes.

o Set up automated alerts to notify administrators of critical errors, changes, or security breaches in real-time.

4. **Access Control and Privilege Management**:

o Automation scripts typically require access to devices and network management systems. It is crucial to follow **principle of least privilege** by granting scripts only the necessary permissions.

o Implement **role-based access control (RBAC)** for network devices and automation platforms to restrict access based on the roles of users and scripts.

o Use **multi-factor authentication (MFA)** for accessing automation systems, especially if they control network infrastructure or handle sensitive data.

Implementing Secure Authentication and Authorization for Automation Scripts

Automation scripts that manage network infrastructure often need to authenticate to devices, APIs, or other services. Implementing secure authentication and authorization practices is essential to ensure that only authorized users and systems can execute automation tasks.

1. **Use Strong Authentication Mechanisms**:
   - o **SSH Keys**: Use SSH keys for authentication rather than passwords. SSH keys are more secure and less susceptible to brute-force attacks. Ensure that private keys are protected with passphrases.
   - o **API Tokens**: Many network platforms (e.g., **SolarWinds, Nagios, PRTG**) use API tokens for authentication. These tokens should be treated like passwords, stored securely, and not exposed in code repositories.
   - o **OAuth**: For systems with OAuth support, such as cloud network platforms, use OAuth tokens for secure authentication. These tokens should be rotated regularly to reduce the risk of token theft.

2. **Secure Credential Storage**:
   - o **Avoid Hardcoding Credentials**: Never hardcode passwords, keys, or API tokens in your

333

automation scripts. Use environment variables or secure vaults for storing credentials.

- ○ **Secrets Management**: Use a **secrets management system** like **HashiCorp Vault**, **AWS Secrets Manager**, or **Azure Key Vault** to securely store and manage sensitive information. These tools provide automatic encryption and access controls to keep secrets safe.
- ○ **Encrypted Configuration Files**: Store network device credentials and other sensitive data in encrypted configuration files. Ensure that only authorized users and automation scripts can decrypt these files.

3. **Use Role-Based Access Control (RBAC)**:
   - ○ **RBAC** ensures that only authorized users or scripts can access specific network resources or execute certain tasks. Define roles such as "read-only", "admin", and "operator", and assign them appropriately to your automation scripts.
   - ○ For example, an automation script used for network monitoring may only require read-only access to devices, whereas a script responsible for applying configuration changes may need administrative privileges. This helps limit the risk if a script is compromised.

4. **Multi-Factor Authentication (MFA)**:

- o Where possible, implement **MFA** for accessing the automation platform or network devices. This adds an extra layer of security, making it harder for attackers to gain access, even if they compromise credentials.
- o Consider using MFA for administrative accounts or for executing high-risk automation tasks like network device configuration.

Avoiding Common Security Risks in Network Automation

While network automation provides tremendous efficiency, it also comes with several security risks. Below are common security risks in network automation and best practices to mitigate them.

1. **Insecure Communication Channels**:
   - o **Risk**: Unencrypted communication between automation scripts and devices exposes sensitive data (e.g., passwords, configuration files) to potential interception.
   - o **Solution**: Always use secure protocols such as **SSH, SFTP, HTTPS**, and **TLS** for communication. Avoid using plain text protocols such as **Telnet** and **HTTP**.

- **Example**: Use **Netmiko** to connect securely to devices via SSH.

```python
python

from netmiko import ConnectHandler

device = {
    'device_type': 'cisco_ios',
    'host': '192.168.1.1',
    'username': 'admin',
    'password': 'password',
    'secret': 'secret',    # Enable password
    'port': 22,
    'verbose': True,
}

net_connect                          =
ConnectHandler(**device)
net_connect.enable()
```

2. **Exposing Sensitive Data in Logs**:
   - **Risk**: Logs may contain sensitive information such as passwords, API tokens, or device details. If logs are exposed or accessed by unauthorized users, this could lead to a security breach.
   - **Solution**:

- Use **log masking** or **redaction** to remove sensitive information from logs.
- Ensure that logs are stored in secure locations with restricted access.
- Use **log rotation** to ensure that logs are archived securely and old logs are deleted after a specified period.

3. **Insufficient Error Handling**:
   - o **Risk**: Automation scripts that don't handle errors properly can lead to inconsistent configurations or security vulnerabilities, especially if errors are silently ignored.
   - o **Solution**:
     - Implement robust **error handling** and **logging** within your scripts to track failures, timeouts, and other issues.
     - Use **try-except** blocks in Python to catch and manage exceptions, ensuring that failures are logged and alert notifications are triggered when necessary.

4. **Configuration Drift**:
   - o **Risk**: Over time, manual changes or inconsistencies between automated and manual configurations can cause "configuration drift," where network devices diverge from the desired configuration.

- o **Solution**:
  - Use **version-controlled configuration files** to ensure that network device configurations are always aligned with the defined standard.
  - Implement **automated configuration validation** scripts to regularly compare actual device configurations against the desired configuration stored in a version control system (e.g., Git).

5. **Inadequate Access Control**:
   - o **Risk**: Automation scripts that execute with overly broad privileges can expose the network to attack if they are compromised.
   - o **Solution**:
     - Always apply the **principle of least privilege** to automation scripts, ensuring they only have access to the resources they need.
     - Implement **RBAC** to control access based on roles and responsibilities, and ensure automation scripts are restricted to necessary tasks.

6. **Lack of Regular Auditing and Updates**:

- o **Risk**: Scripts or network devices may become outdated or vulnerable due to the absence of regular updates or audits.
- o **Solution**:
  - Perform **regular audits** of your automation scripts and network devices to ensure they are secure and up-to-date.
  - Regularly **update Python libraries** and third-party tools used in network automation to patch security vulnerabilities and benefit from performance improvements.

Conclusion

Security is a fundamental aspect of network automation, as automation scripts often have access to critical network configurations and devices. By implementing strong authentication, encrypting sensitive data, and following best practices for access control and error handling, you can mitigate security risks. In addition, regularly auditing your automation scripts, securing communication channels, and ensuring that network configurations are aligned with best practices will help maintain a secure network environment. As the complexity of networks increases, network automation security should always be a top priority to protect against potential vulnerabilities and threats.

CHAPTER 27

THE FUTURE OF NETWORK AUTOMATION

Emerging Trends in Network Automation and AI-Driven Networks

Network automation is continuously evolving, driven by advancements in technology, growing complexity in network infrastructures, and the increasing demand for agility and efficiency. One of the most significant developments in recent years has been the integration of **Artificial Intelligence (AI)** and **Machine Learning (ML)** into network automation. These technologies enable more intelligent and adaptive networks, improving both performance and security.

1. **AI-Driven Network Automation**:

    o **AI-powered Automation**: AI is being integrated into network automation platforms to improve decision-making and network performance. AI can analyze vast amounts of network data, recognize patterns, and make real-time decisions about traffic routing, load balancing, and performance optimization without human intervention.

o **Predictive Analytics**: AI enables predictive analytics that can forecast network failures, detect anomalies, and predict demand surges based on historical data. This helps administrators take preventive actions before problems arise, reducing downtime and improving network reliability.

o **Self-Healing Networks**: AI-driven networks are increasingly able to self-heal, meaning they can automatically detect issues (e.g., network failures, bottlenecks) and make the necessary adjustments, such as rerouting traffic, restarting failed services, or adjusting configurations. This reduces the need for manual intervention and minimizes human error.

o **AI Network Orchestration**: AI helps orchestrate end-to-end automation processes in the network, from provisioning and configuration to monitoring and management, leading to more efficient workflows and faster service delivery.

2. **Network Slicing in 5G**:

o **5G Networks and Automation**: The rollout of 5G networks has led to the concept of **network slicing**, where a physical network is divided into multiple virtual networks (slices), each with its own characteristics and resources. Network automation is crucial to managing these slices, ensuring that each slice meets its unique performance, security, and availability requirements.

o **AI for 5G Management**: AI plays a key role in the management of network slices by dynamically adjusting resources, handling traffic, and ensuring that performance metrics are met for each slice, all without manual intervention.

3. **Edge Computing and Automation**:

o **Edge Computing** is gaining traction as networks move towards decentralized architectures. In edge computing, data processing happens closer to the source (e.g., IoT devices), reducing latency and improving efficiency. Network automation tools are increasingly used to manage edge networks, ensuring seamless connectivity and data processing at scale.

o **AI at the Edge**: AI is being implemented at the edge to improve decision-making and reduce reliance on centralized servers. This enables real-time monitoring, control, and automation of edge devices without needing constant cloud-based intervention.

4. **Network Security Automation with AI**:

- o AI-powered automation is becoming essential in cybersecurity for network management. AI can continuously monitor network traffic, detect malicious activities (e.g., DDoS attacks, unauthorized access), and trigger automatic responses (e.g., blocking malicious IPs, adjusting firewall rules). This proactive approach helps in mitigating threats faster than traditional methods.

The Role of Python in the Future of Network Management

Python has become the de facto programming language for network automation due to its simplicity, versatility, and extensive ecosystem of libraries and frameworks. As network infrastructures grow more complex and automation becomes more integral to network management, Python will continue to play a key role in shaping the future of network management.

1. **Python's Role in AI and ML for Network Automation**:

- o **AI and ML Integration**: Python's rich ecosystem of libraries for AI and machine learning, such as **TensorFlow, Keras, scikit-**

344

learn, and **PyTorch**, will allow network engineers to integrate advanced analytics and machine learning into network automation. With Python, network management systems can evolve from being reactive to proactive, predicting network behavior and automating decisions.

o **Data Processing**: Python will continue to be the go-to tool for processing and analyzing large datasets from network devices and analytics platforms. Libraries like **Pandas**, **NumPy**, and **Matplotlib** are invaluable for data manipulation, statistical analysis, and visualizing network performance.

2. **Enhanced Network Configuration Management**:

o Python will remain an essential tool for configuring and managing network devices. Libraries like **Netmiko**, **Nornir**, and **Napalm** will continue to simplify network configuration management by providing easy-to-use interfaces for interacting with network devices via SSH, API, and other protocols.

o With the rise of **Intent-Based Networking (IBN)**, Python scripts will be used to translate high-level network policies and business intents into device configurations that are automatically deployed, verified, and optimized in real time.

345

3. **Automation and Orchestration**:

- o **Python and Orchestration**: As network automation tools become more sophisticated, Python will be used to orchestrate complex automation workflows across multiple platforms and technologies. Python's ability to integrate with tools like **Ansible, SaltStack,** and **Terraform** will make it easier to automate end-to-end network provisioning, configuration, and monitoring.

- o **Cloud-Native Network Automation**: With the increasing shift toward **cloud-native** network architectures, Python will be essential in managing hybrid and multi-cloud environments. Its ability to interface with cloud APIs (e.g., AWS, Azure, GCP) will make it a key tool in automating cloud networking tasks.

4. **Integration with DevOps Pipelines**:

- o Python will continue to be integrated into **CI/CD pipelines** for network automation, allowing network engineers to automate tasks such as configuration management, testing, and deployment. By using Python in these pipelines, teams can improve the speed and reliability of network updates, reducing the risk of human error and configuration drift.

Preparing for Next-Gen Network Automation

As the landscape of networking evolves with emerging technologies like **5G, SD-WAN**, and **AI-driven networks**, network automation will need to keep pace. Here's how you can prepare for the next generation of network automation:

1. **Investing in AI and Machine Learning Skills**:
   o **AI-Driven Networks**: As AI becomes integral to network management, network engineers should familiarize themselves with machine learning concepts and tools that can be integrated with network automation.
   o **Automation and Data Science**: Understanding how to use **Python** for processing network data and applying machine learning algorithms will be a valuable skill for automating network performance analysis, troubleshooting, and optimization.

2. **Adopting Intent-Based Networking (IBN)**:
   o **IBN** allows network administrators to define high-level business requirements and automatically translate them into network configurations. To leverage IBN effectively, network automation scripts will need to be

347

enhanced with more sophisticated decision-making capabilities, which can be powered by AI.

o Training in IBN technologies, along with the ability to integrate these with existing network automation tools like **Ansible** and **Netmiko**, will be essential.

3. **Focus on Network Security Automation**:

   o **Proactive Security**: With the rise of cyber threats and the increasing complexity of networks, automating network security through AI and Python will become more important. Network engineers should focus on automating threat detection and response using Python and AI tools.

   o Integrating **security monitoring** systems such as **SIEM** (Security Information and Event Management) with Python-based automation scripts will help enhance the security posture of networks in real-time.

4. **Mastering Multi-Cloud and Hybrid Cloud Networks**:

   o As businesses increasingly rely on hybrid and multi-cloud infrastructures, network automation will need to span multiple environments. Python's versatility in cloud orchestration and

348

automation will be crucial to managing these environments effectively.

o Developing skills in integrating cloud APIs with Python scripts will be key to managing complex cloud-native networks.

5. **Prepare for Edge and IoT Network Automation**:

o **Edge Computing** and **IoT** will transform the way networks are managed, with data processing moving closer to the source (e.g., IoT devices, sensors). Automation tools will need to evolve to handle these distributed environments, and Python will play a key role in automating edge network configuration, monitoring, and performance optimization.

6. **Continuous Learning and Adoption of Open-Source Tools**:

o The network automation landscape is constantly evolving, with new tools and technologies emerging regularly. Staying updated on the latest advancements in open-source tools like **Nornir**, **Napalm**, and **Ansible** will help network engineers remain competitive in the field.

o Additionally, understanding and adopting industry best practices for network automation, such as using version control systems, implementing continuous integration, and adopting agile methodologies, will be essential for staying ahead.

Conclusion

The future of network automation is exciting and filled with opportunities. With the integration of AI, machine learning, and cutting-edge technologies like 5G and edge computing, network automation is set to become more intelligent, adaptive, and efficient. Python will continue to be a driving force in network automation, providing the tools needed to integrate these emerging technologies and enable automation at scale. By embracing the latest trends and preparing for next-gen network automation, network professionals can ensure they are well-equipped to manage the future of networking. The key to success lies in continuous learning, adopting new technologies, and leveraging Python's versatility to automate and optimize network management tasks in an increasingly complex landscape.